BLAKE AND THE LANGUAGE OF ART

JANET A. WARNER

Blake and the Language of Art

McGILL-QUEEN'S UNIVERSITY PRESS
Kingston and Montreal

ALAN SUTTON
Gloucester

ISBN 0-7735-0435-4
Legal deposit 4th quarter 1984
Bibliothèque nationale du Québec
Printed in Canada

First published in Great Britain in 1984 by
Alan Sutton Publishing Company Limited
30 Brunswick Road
Gloucester GL1 1JJ
ISBN 0-86299-205-2

Canadian Cataloguing in Publication Data

Warner, Janet A. (Janet Adele), 1931–
Blake and the language of art

Includes bibliographical references and index.
ISBN 0-7735-0435-4

1. Blake, William, 1757–1827. I. Title.

N6797.B57W37 1984 709'.2'4 C84-098984-9

This book has been published with the help of a grant from the Canadian Federation for the Humanities, using funds provided by the Social Sciences and Humanities Research Council of Canada. Publication has also been assisted by the Canada Council under its block grant program.

FOR JOHN, RENÉE, AND PAUL

Contents

Illustrations

Illustrations

Abbreviations

E David V. Erdman, ed., *The Complete Poetry and Prose of William Blake* (Berkeley and Los Angeles: University of California Press 1982).

Butlin Martin Butlin, *The Paintings and Drawings of William Blake*, 2 vols.: *Text* and *Plates* (New Haven and London: Yale University Press 1981).

Night Thoughts Designs for Edward Young's *The Complaint and the Consolation: or Night Thoughts*.

NT Plates in *William Blake's Designs for Edward Young's Night Thoughts*, ed. David V. Erdman, John E. Grant, Edward J. Rose, Michael J. Tolley, 2 vols. (Oxford: Clarendon 1980).

Roe Albert S. Roe, *Blake's Illustrations to the Divine Comedy* (Princeton: Princeton University Press 1953).

Vala G.E. Bentley, Jr, ed., *Vala or The Four Zoas* (Oxford: Clarendon 1963).

ARO *All Religions Are One*

BL *The Book of Los*

BU *The Book of Urizen*

FZ *The Four Zoas*

J *Jerusalem*

M *Milton*

MHH *The Marriage of Heaven and Hell*

Thel *The Book of Thel*

TNR *There Is No Natural Religion*

VDA *Visions of the Daughters of Albion*

VLJ *A Vision of the Last Judgment*

NUMBERING SYSTEMS

Blake's unique method of engraving both words and designs together on copper plates, making the printed page simultaneously a design and a text, creates special problems when one needs to refer to particular sections of a given work. Here, as in most books about Blake, a combination of roman and arabic numbers are used as aids to location. I have also made the distinction between text and designs for the *Four Zoas* manuscript by locating the text in E and referring to it as FZ, but using *Vala* when discussing designs, referring to the facsimile edition edited by G.E. Bentley, Jr.

Roman numerals indicate the chapter, or "Night," divisions of Blake's poetry and designs; thus (FZ v: 61; E 341) means *The Four Zoas*, Night Five, manuscript page 61, E page 341. Similarly (*Vala* IV: 47) refers to the design in the facsimile edition.

Arabic numbers indicate plate or page or line numbers of Blake's works; for example (*J* 74: 4–9) means *Jerusalem*, plate 74, lines 4–9. In the case of designs for *Night Thoughts*, arabic numbers refer to the numbering system of the Clarendon edition; thus (Night IV: *NT* 114) means Night Four, number 114, in *William Blake's Designs for Edward Young's Night Thoughts*, ed. Erdman et al. (Oxford: Clarendon 1980).

Preface

In these books the same attitudes and movements appear again and again. It is the weak side of Blake's art ... . We forgive the endless repetitions of attitude and gesture because of the genius which has made them rush, and float, and fly through the air, embrace with ecstasy or collapse in despair.
– Laurence Binyon, *The Engraved Designs of William Blake*, 1926

Painting admits not a Grain of Sand or a Blade of Grass Insignificant much less an Insignificant Blur or Mark.
– Blake, *A Vision of the Last Judgment*

Reading William Blake's pictures is a different experience from reading his poetry. It is, for one thing, easier, because he provides us with more clues.

This statement may seem heretical in the recent milieu of Blake criticism, which sees an increasingly more complex and difficult Blake, a Blake whose "sister arts" are working independently, if not at cross purposes. Yet Geoffrey Hartman remarked at a conference on Blake and Criticism (at the University of California, Santa Cruz, in May 1982) that while there were some things about Blake that were known and understood, there was also that category of what was *not known*, but understood. This is why a perceptive reader will always find Blake's work rewarding (for intuition is one's greatest aid in interpreting Blake, even when one is a seasoned scholar), and the designs can be the key which unlocks the treasure chest. In this book, my approach to Blake is from design to poetry, rather than the other way around. For quite early in his career as an artist Blake developed a set of visual forms, gestures and attitudes of the human body, which he came to use repeatedly. Though both art and literary critics have regarded these repeated forms with some embarrassment and there is a continuing lively discussion about their meaning, Blake undoubtedly perceived archetypes of gesture and stance in the work of painters and sculptors, and used them in his own art as a kind of visual vocabulary.

In this book I call Blake's repetition of visual images a pictorial language, sometimes a language complementary to the poetry, yet often suggestive, in W.J.T. Mitchell's phrase, of the *world of pictures*, of the language of art which exists to extend the medium of speech by a kind of visual shorthand. My aim is to demonstrate the variety and importance of this language, amplifying work which I began some years ago when I first became acquainted with the world of Blake's images. These images of the human body constitute a visual vocabulary which often works in conjunction with his verbal text, and sometimes without it, to underline the important concepts of Humanity, Form, and Energy which all Blake readers must strive to understand.

Blake's "borrowings" from earlier art and his use of "the great traditions to which he was heir" have, since the 1940s, been documented principally by Anthony Blunt, Collins Baker, Jean Hagstrum, Bo Lindberg, and David Bindman. These scholars have shown how Blake became familiar with classical art through engravings after Raphael, Michelangelo, and Giulio Romano and that he adapted from Salviati, Caracci, Scamozzi, and from Flaxman, Romney, and Fuseli. Scholars have, in fact, proved Blake familiar with a singularly wide range of artistic works and traditions. Demonstrating that he took over these images, critics point out that Blake learned figure-drawing by such copying and then pay tribute to his capacity for "breathing living flame into driest bones." And while several conjecture the processes of Blake's imagination and sensitively show Blake in relation to the artistic heritage of the eighteenth century, few other than Bo Lindberg have suggested that there may be essential reasons for his use of the same images again and again. Lindberg's important study, *William Blake's Illustrations to the Book of Job*, used Aby Warburg's term *pathos formula* to categorize visual symbols. To what extent Blake's formula-figures stand alone as symbols and to what extent their meanings are defined by the context in which they appear is a central concern of the following chapters. To turn the pages of the magnificent catalogue raisonné of Blake's work by Martin Butlin, *The Paintings and Drawings of William Blake*, is to realize just how frequently Blake repeated his motifs. The recent work which attempts the most comprehensive account of Blake's composite art is W.J.T. Mitchell's book of that title, a brilliant and suggestive book which states in a theoretical early chapter that "the recurrent figural motif does not in itself have any denotative meaning."[1]

My approach, it will be evident, assumes a firmly persuaded Blake who did intend certain figures and stances of the human body to carry a nucleus of meaning, to be the components of a language in which "every Word & Every Character Was Human" (*J* 98). I use the terms *visual image* and *visual form* to refer to the art object and to distinguish it from a mental image produced by a poetic text. I have not used the vocabulary of semiotics except in so far as some of it was instinctive. Semiology deals with similar relationships of image and meaning and gestural code, and a more theoretical study than mine may find in Blake's artistic systems a fruitful field of application. Yet because structuralist criticism on the whole has an even more impenetrable style than Blake criticism, the combination could be daunting.

This book is divided into two sections: the first concerns general background, the second specific studies of four visual forms. In my Introduction, the milieu out of which Blake drew his images is sketched (with attention paid in the Appendix to the decorative arts). Chapter 1 discusses Blake's ideas of Eternal Form and Fallen Form. Chapter 2 surveys the kinds of visual languages that interested the late eighteenth century – the Passions, as codified in essays on gesture, acting, and pantomime – and links them to Blake's work. In the second section of the book, each of the four chapters illustrates the way an important Blakean idea has realized itself in a visual symbol.

Parts of the Introduction to Part 1 of this book appeared originally in "Blake and the Language of Art," *Colby Library Quarterly* 13 (June 1977), and the Appendix to Part 1 in "Blake and English Printed Textiles," *Blake Newsletter* (Spring 1973). In chapter 3, the section on the outstretched arms, which was first published with extended footnotes and an appendix in *Blake's Visionary Forms Dramatic*, ed. David V. Erdman and John E. Grant, copyright (©) 1970 by Princeton University Press, is adapted by permission of Princeton University Press. Chapter 6 first appeared in *William Blake: Essays in Honour of Sir Geoffrey Keynes*, ed. Morton D. Paley and Michael Phillips (Oxford: Clarendon 1973).

For research and travel grants which enabled me to write this book, I am grateful for the generous support of the Social Sciences and Humanities Research Council of Canada and the Research Grants Committee of Glendon College, York University.

Colleagues and fellow Blake scholars have also been generous with their time and interest: I am grateful to Gerald E. Bentley, Jr, Morris Eaves, David V. Erdman, Christopher Heppner, Robert Simmons, and John Sutherland. My graduate students at York University, especially James Boyd Brown, have been a source of insight and stimulating conversation. Many happy hours have been spent in research libraries in England and the United States: I appreciate especially the gracious assistance of librarians of the Huntington Library, San Marino, California. Curators of the British Museum Print Room, the Metropolitan Museum of Art Print Room, the Fitzwilliam Museum and the Lawrence Lande Blake Collection in the Department of Rare Books and Special Collections, McLennan Library, McGill University, have been unfailingly helpful on repeated visits over the years. I am grateful too for the hospitality of three people who generously share their private collections with visiting scholars: Robert Essick, George Goyder, and the late Sir Geoffrey Keynes. My thanks go also to John Warner, who began it all by taking me to the Blake exhibition in London in 1957, and to Northrop Frye, who introduced me to Blake's poetry. To my friend Christopher Heppner I owe a special debt of gratitude and affection. For help with preparation of the manuscript my thanks to Stuart Broomer, Ann Russell, and especially Beryl Logan, who typed the manuscript through all its Forms, Fallen and Eternal.

J.W.
Glendon College
York University, Toronto

PART I

THE LANGUAGE OF ART

INTRODUCTION

A Heritage of Images

In May of 1809 William Blake presented to the public an exhibition of his "Giant Forms." The house of his brother James at 28 Broad Street in London was used as a gallery, and Blake issued for the occasion his own *Descriptive Catalogue*, as well as four advertising pamphlets. The sixteen pictures represented "The grand style of Art restored, in Fresco or Water-colour Painting,"[1] and included *The Canterbury Pilgrims* and the two pictures of the "Spiritual Forms" of Nelson and Pitt, as well as *The Ancient Britons*, an important picture representing "the Strongest Man, the Beautifullest Man, and the Ugliest Man," which has been lost.[2] Whatever Blake's hopes for personal recognition through his exhibition may have been, it was most certainly a political gesture.[3] It could hardly have been otherwise for a man who wrote that "The Arts & Sciences are the Destruction of Tyrannies or Bad Governments ... The Foundation of Empire is Art & Science Remove them or Degrade them & the Empire is No More – Empire follows Art & not Vice Versa as Englishmen suppose."[4] His advertisement for the exhibition outlines his invention of portable frescos which could be exhibited as wall panels in public buildings; as Raphael and Michelangelo had "enriched and made great" Italy by fresco, so Blake would do for England: "if Art is the glory of a Nation, if Genius and Inspiration are the great Origin and Bond of Society, the distinction my Works have obtained from those who best understand such things, calls for my Exhibition as the greatest of Duties to my Country" (E 528).

In Blake's view, the decline of artistic taste in England (reflected by the popularity of Reynolds and Gainsborough, who "Blotted and Blurred"), had direct bearing on England's state as an empire (or tyranny) at war with Napoleon. There were men who "would if they could, for ever depress Mental & prolong Corporeal War ... a Class of Men whose whole delight is in Destroying."[5] In the preface to *Milton*, whose words I have just quoted, Blake called upon painters, sculptors, and architects to rebel against the neoclassicism ("Greek or Roman models") of the age.[6] This was the spirit which was suppressing true imaginative expression and desolating Europe with wars,[7] for neoclassicism encouraged a dangerous form of abstraction, a dependence on public rules rather than private inspiration. ("One Law for the Lion & Ox is Oppression," he had written in *The Marriage of Heaven and Hell.*) Blake's fervent desire in *Milton* that all men would be prophets is reiterated in his call to Englishmen to be art critics: "O Englishmen! know that every man ought to be a judge of pictures, and every man is so who has not been connoisseured out of his senses."[8]

Blake's prefaces to *Milton* and *Jerusalem*, the *Descriptive Catalogue*, and the *Notebook* entries known as his "Public Address" were all directed to the English public, in which Blake had a touching faith: "I say the English Public are true Encouragers of real Art while they discourage & look with contempt on False Art."[9] It would be easy to dismiss some of this as the wishful thinking of a lonely artist who has faith in his own work were it not for Blake's essentially practical knowledge that he spoke through his art a common language that all men could understand.[10] Blake's perception of this language of the archetypes of gesture and stance used by painters and sculptors was transformed in his own work into highly

1 (below) Cartari, *Imagini:* Apollo figure
2 (right) Dürer, *Apollo and Diana*

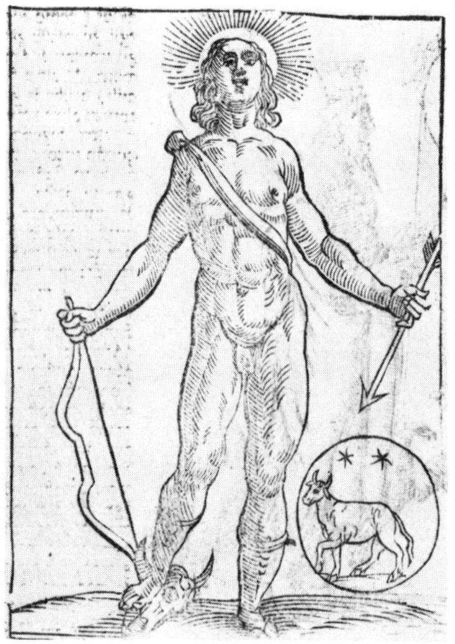

sophisticated pictorial language, which he had every reason to believe his public would recognize. For all around them were signs and symbols on shops and inns, on trade cards, on flags and heraldic badges, on embroidery patterns and textiles, and in all manner of applied arts such as ceramics and furniture decoration. And while all this was available to the general public, men and women of education had even greater sources of symbolic material at their command.

The study of the history of iconography is a relatively modern discipline, but it has already demonstrated the great continuity of visual symbol which existed well into the seventeenth century, surviving in neoclassical transformations in Blake's time.[11] A main repository of these symbols – which are in general representations of human and animal forms as allegorical figures – are the emblem books and the manuals of sixteenth-century mythographers. These were the sources for the *Iconologia* of Cesare Ripa,[12] the monumental work which became a bible of symbols for European art. It first appeared in Rome in 1593, going through many editions and translations. It was published first in England in 1709 and would also have been known to Blake in editions of 1777–9. There was also a 1778 edition by George Richardson, the complete title of which is worth quoting as an indication of its contents:

Iconology, or, a Collection of Emblematical Figures, moral and instructive; exhibiting the images of the elements and celestial bodies, the seasons and months of the year, the principal rivers, the Four Ages, the Muses, the Senses, Arts, Sciences, Dispositions and Faculties of the mind, virtues and vices. Containing, in four books, upwards of four hundred and twenty remarkable subjects, engraved from Original designs, with particular explanation of the figures, their attributes and symbols illustrated by a variety of authorities from classical authors, selected and composed from the most approved emblematical representations of the ancient compositions of Cavaliere Cesare Ripa, Perugino.

Besides the *Iconologia*, one of the most influential of the mythographer's manuals was Vincenzo Cartari's *Imagini Delli Dei Gl'Antichi* (1556), published in England without illustrations as *The Fountain of Ancient Fiction, wherein is lively depictured the images of the gods of the ancients* (London 1599). An Apollo figure Blake used consistently likely came to him via Dürer after Cartari (see figures 1–5). There were also the books of the English emblem writers Franchis Quarles, John Wynne, and George Wither. Blake's use of these English emblemists has been – and continues to be – explored by Hagstrum and others.[13] Piloo Nanavutty, in an early study of Blake and the emblems, noted that it was those images which had "a wide currency in the general iconographic tradition" that Blake tended to use.[14]

A lesser-known but equally important tradition, which is explored in chapter 2, is the tradition of the language of gesture used by orators, actors, and artists. This tradition stemmed from a Renaissance work by

3 Blake, *Satan in His Original Glory*

Heritage Images

4 Blake, *Milton*, plate 16

5 Blake, design for Edward Young's *Night Thoughts* 246

(25)

And wander wild, through Things impossible!
What *Wealth*, in *Faculties* of endless growth,
In quenchless *Passions* violent to crave,
In *Liberty* to chuse, in *Power* to reach,
And in *Duration* (how thy Riches rise?)
Duration to perpetuate------ boundless Bliss?
 Ask you, what *Power* resides in feeble Man
That Bliss to gain? Is *Virtue*'s, then, unknown?
Virtue, our present Peace, our future Prize.
Man's unprecarious, natural Estate,
Improveable at will, in Virtue, lies;
Its Tenure sure; its Income is Divine.
 High-built Abundance, heap on heap! for what?
To breed new wants, and beggar us the more;
Then, make a richer Scramble for the Throng?
Soon as this feeble Pulse, which leaps so long
Almost by Miracle, is tir'd with play,
Like Rubbish, from disploding Engines thrown,
Our Magazines of hoarded Trifles fly;
Fly diverse; fly to Foreigners, to Foes;

E New

John Bulwer, *Chirologia: or the Natural Language of the Hand* (1644). Added to this was the influence of Charles LeBrun's *A Method to Learn to Design the Passions* (1734).

Blake's knowledge of these traditions would have begun early, at Henry Pars's drawing school, where he was sent at the age of ten. There drawing was taught by copying plaster casts of the antique and by making copies of prints and drawings. Copying was therefore for him and others the grammar of the language of art and lies behind such statements as:

To learn the Language of Art Copy for Ever. is my Rule (*Annotations to Reynolds*, E 636).

The difference between a bad Artist & a Good One Is the Bad Artist Seems to Copy a Great Deal: The Good one Really Does Copy a Great Deal (*Annotations to Reynolds*, E 645).

Blake therefore could and did take most of Western art (and also what Eastern art he knew of, such as E. Moor's *Hindu Pantheon*) for his province, and his use of images other artists had used was his way of affirming the unity of the human imagination. "What is Laying up materials but Copying" he asked.[15] Furthermore, the English artists of Blake's day were continually using the same motifs. Anthony Blunt's comment that "there were certain motives and certain images which were, one might almost say, the common property of the whole group to which Blake, Fuseli, Flaxman, Romney and Stothard belonged ... each member of the group produced his own particular interpretation of the motive"[16] underlines the assumption by those artists of an artistic language, though Blunt himself spends some pages discussing the question of "borrowing" or plagiarizing before concluding that the question of priority is a futile argument.[17] Joseph Burke's important article "The Eidetic and The Borrowed Image" (1964), which traces the phenomenon graphically, surprisingly concludes that Blake's borrowings could seldom have been deliberate but were rather the unconscious product of his eidetic imagination.[18] More recently, however, Robert Rosenblum has demonstrated that certain classical items and motifs appear again and again in late eighteenth-century art, with visual similarities that can mean that one artist is in fact consciously commenting on the statement of another.[19] Rosenblum's many examples of deathbed motifs include Blake's *Breach in a City the Morning after the Battle* and the title-page to *Songs of Experience*, which Rosenblum compares with designs of Romney and Flaxman. Other examples may be found, for example, in illustrations to Milton by the same group, Barry, Fuseli, Lawrence, and Blake. Furthermore, there was a tradition of borrowings even among the most famous artists of the day, including Benjamin West, Joshua Reynolds, and William Hogarth, which modern art historians discuss actively.

Bo Lindberg, in his study of the *Job* designs, has found that

attitudes or gestures embodying a special meaning in one work of art, tend to carry this same meaning in other works by the same artist or by another. That is: they have a conventional meaning. Artists use *pathos-formulae* as writers use words; and like the meaning of a word, the meaning of a pathos-formula can be modified or altered by context. The study of these formulae is the lexicography of art ... (page 115)

Once he had chosen his own visual vocabulary from this lexicography, Blake used it consistently, as the second part of this book intends to demonstrate. On the domestic scene, designers of plate-printed cotton and ceramic designers copied popular artists' engravings for their designs for textiles and pottery (see Appendix to Part 1). With so much of this around him, no wonder Blake could speak of a language of Art, born of Copying. To put these visual symbols in the context of the arts of Blake's time and to show how a nucleus of visual symbols amplifies Blake's poetic text is the aim of this and the following chapters.

FROM COPY TO VISION

The heritage of images from the antique and the exchange of motifs among contemporary eighteenth-century painters were factors which encouraged Blake in a Neoplatonic idealism which underlies his ideas of art, for Blake believed that the images of art came not from nature but from imagination. When, as a mature artist, he wrote down the principles implicit in all his work, his pronouncements clearly indicated his awareness of the differences between his own aesthetic orientation and the prevailing criticism:

No Man of Sense ever supposes that Copying from Nature is the Art of Painting ("Public Address," E 578).

There Exist in that Eternal World the Permanent Realities of Every Thing which we see reflected in this Vegetable Glass of Nature (*VLJ*, E 555).

Men think they can Copy Nature as Correctly as I copy Imagination this they will find Impossible. & all the Copies or Pretended Copiers of Nature from Rembrat to Reynolds Prove that Nature becomes [tame] to its Victim nothing but Blots & Blurs. Why are Copiers of Nature Incorrect while Copiers of Imagination are Correct this is manifest to all ("Public Address," E 574–5).

These excerpts demonstrate that Blake was describing the copying of something quite distinct from the external world. The "vegetable glass of Nature" is only the mirror of the external images; art is the "correct" copying of Imagination, the home of "Permanent Reality."

This idea, so basic to Blake's concept of art, is essentially Neoplatonic. Plato's distrust of art had been amended by Neoplatonists, who contended that the artist bypassed nature and imitated directly the original "Ideas" of perfection.[20] Though critics are divided about the extent and form of Platonic and Neoplatonic influence in Blake's poetry, its effect on his aesthetic is clear. *Imaginative form* is a term he used as late as 1820 (in an annotation to Berkeley's *Siris*) to mean the "reality" of a thing, as George Mills Harper has noted in his book *The Neoplatonism of William Blake*.[21] This, as Harper comments, is a Platonic statement written after many years of anti-Greek statements on Blake's part, indicating that Platonic aesthetics remained with him. Harper does not discuss Blake's visual images to any extent, and this remark has seldom been investigated by critics other than Kathleen Raine, whose extreme Neoplatonic bias has irritated many scholars. Nevertheless, Blake's brand of Neoplatonism is generally recognized as having been filtered through a probable reading of Thomas Taylor's translations of Plato. In my view, Blake's belief in imaginative form lies behind the repeated figures and gestures used in a symbolic manner and shared with other artists. Of course, for Blake, the language of visual images is man-made, not God-given, and the visual symbols as he recognized them have not the static nature associated with Platonic eternal form. Confusion arises when Blake's "critical" Platonic language in the prose (for example, in the Chaucer Prospectus) confronts the dynamic metaphors in the poetry, as when the Eternal Forms "walked To and fro in Eternity." In his designs the energy of the visual image is suggested by variation of detail or context. Yet no matter how originally or idiosyncratically Blake used visual images, he was always aware of the traditional importance that could be attached to symbolic images. They were the nucleus of meanings – the cornerstones of inspiration.

There was, however, the problem of obscurity to contend with. In the Renaissance, mythological and symbolic images had become surrounded by mysterious allegorical explanations which often were so esoteric that few could understand them. The early eighteenth century favoured a more empirical approach, which sought to confine allegory to images readily understood.[22] Therefore, the didactic or representational image of which the eighteenth century was so fond was something of a protest against the obscurity of the emblems which Neoplatonism had implied were always more than mere representation. E.H. Gombrich refers to the Neoplatonic conception of symbolism as a "form of revelation,"[23] and indeed this is basically Blake's attitude, as we know from his words in *A Vision of the Last Judgment*:

> If the Spectator could Enter into these Images in his Imagination approaching them on the Fiery Chariot of his Contemplative Thought if he could Enter into Noahs Rainbow or into his bosom or could make a Friend & Companion of one of these Images of wonder which always intreats him to leave mortal things as he

must know then would he arise from his Grave then would he meet the Lord in the Air & then he would be happy (E 560).

The key word here, of course, is "Enter"; the images are not merely representations but possess a power of their own, close to a physical existence, an extension of the Christian word made flesh. Gombrich, in *Symbolic Images*, discusses a speech in praise of certain emblematic figures by a teacher of rhetoric, Christophoro Giarda (delivered in 1626, but reproduced in 1725, in Latin, in Graevius' *Thesaurus Antiquitatum*), which may or may not have been known to Blake[24] but is sufficiently relevant to the above passage in *A Vision of the Last Judgment* to justify quoting:

As nothing can be apprehended by the senses that is not somewhat corporeal, nothing can be understood by our mind in its depressed condition that has not the appearance of a body. Who, then, can sufficiently estimate the magnitude of the debt we owe to those who expressed the Arts and Sciences themselves in images and thus achieved it that we can not only know them but look at them, as it were, with our eyes, that we can meet them and almost converse with them about a variety of matters?[25]

The blurring of the distinction between symbol and reality which we recognize here is found in Blake's words also and is typical of Renaissance art, where abstract ideas such as chastity or penitence may be painted as real and visible or where the great baroque ceiling-paintings of Heaven are intended to create an illusion so vivid that the painted heaven can evoke the ecstatic response of religious vision.

Blake's defence of his own technique is based on this tradition:

The connoisseurs and artists who have made objections to Mr. B's mode of representing spirits with real bodies, would do well to consider that the Venus, the Minerva, the Jupiter, the Apollo, which they admire in Greek statues, are all of them representations of spiritual existences of God's immortal, to the mortal perishing organ of sight; and yet they are embodied and organized in solid marble. Mr. B. requires the same latitude and all is well. The Prophets describe what they saw in Vision as real and existing men whom they saw with their imaginative and immortal organs; the Apostles the same; the clearer the organ the more distinct the object. A Spirit and a Vision are not, as the modern philosophy supposes, a cloudy vapour or a nothing: they are organized and minutely articulated beyond all that the mortal and perishing nature can produce. (*A Descriptive Catalogue*, E 541)

Here Blake emphasizes the special reality and clarity of imaginative images (as he does so often in other places also); their qualities as agents of revelation he underlines in *VLJ* when he states that his work is an "Endeavour to Restore what the Ancients called the Golden Age" (E 555). For Blake, then, images of art were both revelatory and clear, and thus that part of traditional lore which surrounded them in mystery he dismissed. He could therefore understand the contemporary desire for rationality in allegorical imagery, but he could see that the attempt had led society to *generalize*, much to its detriment. Commenting on the aesthetics of Reynolds, he rails: "To Generalize is to be an Idiot To Particularize is the Alone Distinction of Merit" (E 641). Generalizing made the language of art into illustrated metaphor rather than revelation, and he must have recognized that much vitality had gone from the execution of many traditional emblems. In the Prospectus to Robert Blair's *The Grave* (1805), Robert Hartley Cromek touched upon this problem and recognized Blake's achievement in design:

The Importance of this Object has been so well understood at every Period of Time, from the earliest and most innocent, to the latest and most depraved, that Reason and Fancy have exhausted their Stores of Argument and Imagery, to impress it on the Mind: animate and inanimate Nature, the Seasons, the Forest and the Field, the Bee and Ant, the Larva, Crysalis and Moth, have lent their real or supposed Analogies with the Origin, Pursuits, and End, of the Human Race, so often to emblematic Purposes, that Instruction is become stale, and Attention callous. The Serpent with its Tail in its Mouth, from a Type of Eternity, is become an Infant's Bauble; even the nobler Idea of Hercules pausing between Virtue and Vice, or the varied Imagery of Death leading his Patients to the Grave, owe their Effect upon us more to technic Excellence than allegoric Utility.

Aware of this, but conscious that Affection of Originality and trite Repetition would equally impede his Success, the Author of the Moral Series before us, has endeavoured to wake Sensibility by touching our Sympathies with nearer, less ambiguous, and less ludicrous Imagery, than what Mythology, Gothic Superstition, or Symbols as far-fetched as inadequate could supply. His Invention has been chiefly employed to spread a familiar and domestic Atmosphere round the most important of all Subjects, to connect the visible and the invisible World, without provoking Probability, and to lead the Eye from the milder Light of Time to the Radiations of Eternity.[26]

Similarly, verbal allegory was often debased; Blake eventually made a distinction between "Allegory or Fable" and true vision: "Vision or Imagination is a Representation of what Eternally exists. Really & Unchangeably. Fable or Allegory is Formd by the daughters of Memory. Imagination is Surrounded by the daughters of Inspiration ..." (*VLJ*, E 554).

Memory, which is part of our ability to generalize, has no part in helping us grasp the true meanings of images. Blake here implies the power of the symbol to be apprehended in a flash of understanding.[27] The visual image is an immediate perception – it is not a memory. None of Blake's paintings is a memory of what he has seen – they are the real thing, each time you look at them.[28] Re-creations, not imitations; although there may be "correct" copying, for that is visionary. Blake is careful to make the distinction between copying and imitation: "To recover Art has been the business of my life to the Florentine Original & if possible to go beyond that Original ... To Imitate I abhore I obstinately

6 Blake, *Jerusalem*, plate 63

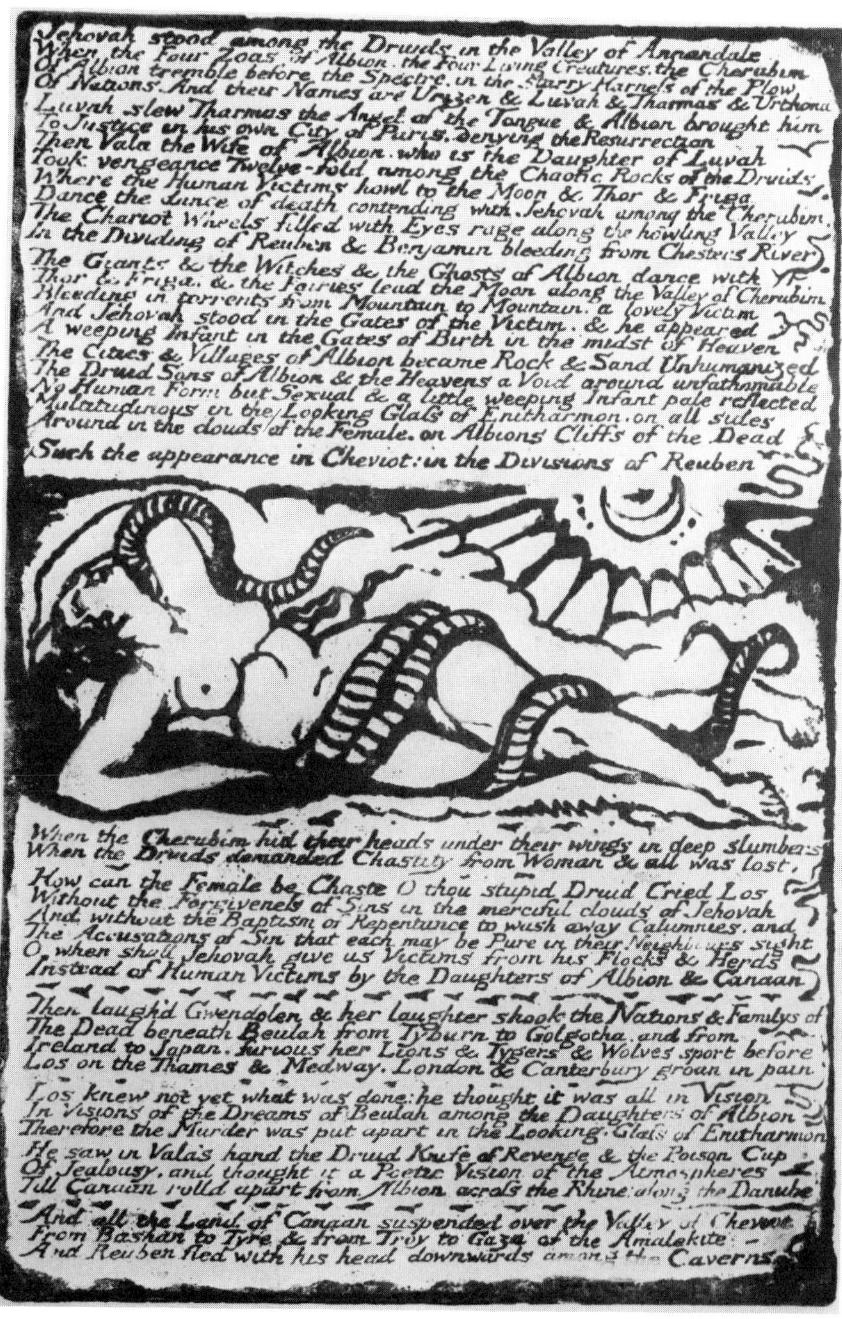
Jehovah stood among the Druids in the Valley of Annandale
When the Four Zoas of Albion. the Four Living Creatures. the Cherubim
Of Albion tremble before the Spectre. in the Starry Harness of the Plow
Of Nations. And their Names are Urizen & Luvah & Tharmas & Urthona
Luvah slew Tharmas the Angel of the Tongue & Albion brought him
To Justice in his own City of Paris. denying the Resurrection
Then Vala the Wife of Albion. who is the Daughter of Luvah
Took vengeance Twelve-fold among the Chaotic Rocks of the Druids
Where the Human Victims howl to the Moon & Thor & Friga
Dance the dance of death contending with Jehovah among the Cherubim.
The Chariot Wheels filled with Eyes rage along the howling Valley
In the Dividing of Reuben & Benjamin bleeding from Chesters River
The Giants & the Witches & the Ghosts of Albion dance with
Thor & Friga. & the Fairies lead the Moon along the Valley of Cherubim
Bleeding in torrents from Mountain to Mountain. a lovely Victim
And Jehovah stood in the Gates of the Victim. & he appeared
A weeping Infant in the Gates of Birth in the midst of Heaven
The Cities & Villages of Albion became Rock & Sand Unhumanized
The Druid Sons of Albion & the Heavens a Void around unfathomable
No Human Form but Sexual & a little weeping Infant pale reflected
Multitudinous in the Looking Glass of Enitharmon. on all sides
Around in the clouds of the Female. on Albions Cliffs of the Dead
Such the appearance in Cheviot: in the Divisions of Reuben

When the Cherubim hid their heads under their wings in deep slumbers
When the Druids demanded Chastity from Woman & all was lost.
How can the Female be Chaste O thou stupid Druid Cried Los
Without the Forgiveness of Sins in the merciful clouds of Jehovah
And without the Baptism of Repentance to wash away Calumnies. and
The Accusations of Sin that each may be Pure in their Neighbours sight
O when shall Jehovah give us Victims from his Flocks & Herds
Instead of Human Victims by the Daughters of Albion & Canaan

Then laugh'd Gwendolen, & her laughter shook the Nations & Familys of
The Dead beneath Beulah from Tyburn to Golgotha. and from
Ireland to Japan. furious her Lions & Tygers & Wolves sport before
Los on the Thames & Medway. London & Canterbury groan in pain

Los knew not yet what was done: he thought it was all in Vision
In Visions of the Dreams of Beulah among the Daughters of Albion
Therefore the Murder was put apart in the Looking-Glass of Enitharmon
He saw in Vala's hand the Druid Knife of Revenge & the Poison Cup
Of Jealousy. and thought it a Poetic Vision of the Atmospheres
Till Canaan rolld apart from Albion across the Rhine: along the Danube

And all the Land of Canaan suspended over the Valley of Cheviot
From Bashan to Tyre & from Troy to Gaza of the Amalekite
And Reuben fled with his head downwards among the Caverns

7 Ariadne

8 Figure of Cleopatra

adhere to the true Style of Art such as Michael Angelo Rafael Jul Rom Alb Durer left it (the art of Invention not of Imitation). Imagination is My World ..." ("Public Address," E 580). So we realize that to copy "the true style of art" is not to imitate but rather to re-invent. For art is not progressive. Blake writes: "If Art was Progressive We should have had Mich Angelo's & Rafaels to Succeed & to Improve upon each other But it is not so" (E 656).

Our modern conception of "borrowings" in Blake's art, therefore, implies more censure than it should, for he knew well what he was doing. His own copying of images was in his mind different from the neoclassical idea of imitation, which meant generalizing or abstracting the truth of an image, blurring and blotting out the essential particular form. Proper Copying or Invention meant rediscovery, an individual and particular starting point.

Blake uses a familiar visual image not as an unchangeable icon but rather as a nucleus which may have accrued meanings over the years as other artists employed it. One of his most striking designs – plate 63 of *Jerusalem* (figure 6) – has a most impressive iconographical lineage, and

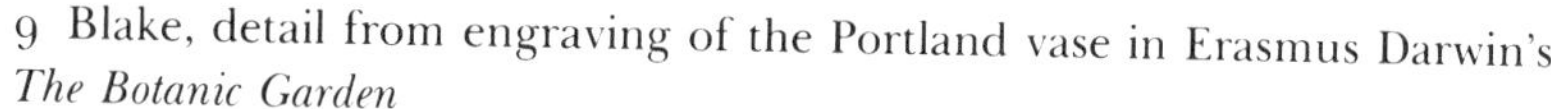

9 Blake, detail from engraving of the Portland vase in Erasmus Darwin's *The Botanic Garden*

to trace it briefly here will demonstrate again how Blake made use of the language of art, providing a new context for a traditional image.

THE ARIADNE FIGURE

Jerusalem 63 is dominated by the seductive reclining figure of a female nude in an attitude of ecstasy, her left arm raised over her head, which is thrown back. Her figure is wound about with a worm. The text of the preceding plate for the most part concerns Vala and her daughters, "the Seed of Woman," and plate 63 continues to describe her vengeance in terms of Druid sacrifice and a dance of death:

> Such the appearance of Cheviot: in the Divisions of Reuben
> When the Cherubim hid their heads under their wings in deep slumbers
> When the Druids demanded Chastity from Woman & all was lost.
> How can the Female be Chaste O thou stupid Druid Cried Los (E 214).

I think that the illustration on plate 63 is a comment on these lines, the

10 George Cumberland, *Thoughts on Outline*, plate 1: *Psyche Disobeys*

reclining nude and worm reminding us of the sexuality of all nature, the impossibility (and even undesirability) of chastity in the natural world. The combination of the sun and the moon in one emblem further underlines the meaning of nature here. (Blake often uses familiar though not identical reclining females to represent the female principle.)

Blake's reclining nude here is an image which resonates with associations throughout art history. It began as a Dionysiac nude, a sculptured nereid often appearing on ancient sarcophagi. Sometimes the figure is identified as Ariadne discovered by Bacchus. In Greek mythology, Ariadne was the daughter of Minos, king of Crete, who aided Theseus in slaying the Minotaur by giving him a ball of string to help him find his way out of the Labyrinth. She escaped Crete with Theseus, but he abandoned her on the isle of Naxos, where Bacchus, discovering her asleep,

11 Titian, *Bacchanal*

Heritage Images

fell in love with her and made her his bride.[29] Blake may have had this myth in mind when he wrote in *J* 77: "I give you the end of a golden string, / Only wind it into a ball: / It will lead you in at Heavens gate, / Built in Jerusalems Wall" (E 231).

There is an antique sculpture called the Ariadne of the Vatican (second century BC) discovered in the sixteenth century (figure 7) and thought in the eighteenth to be Cleopatra. It was copied in a charming eighteenth-century ceramic figurine called Cleopatra (figure 8). Blake may have known a drawing by Raphael of the Ariadne sculpture in Rome.[30] He had engraved Stothard's *Callisto*, which borrowed the form. Certainly, however, he was familiar with the reclining figure on the Portland vase which he engraved for Erasmus Darwin's *Botanic Garden* in 1791 (figure 9).[31] Blake also engraved a rather similar reclining figure –

12 Rubens, *Bacchanal*

but this time a boy – in 1794 for George Cumberland's *Thoughts on Outline*; the design was of the sleeping Cupid discovered by Psyche (figure 10).

Blake's immediate source for his Jerusalem nude, however, could have been Titian's *Bacchanal* (or *The Andrians*) – in Kenneth Clark's opinion one of the most splendid nudes of the High Renaissance (figure 11). Or, if Blake did not know the Titian, he could have known a copy – the Rubens *Bacchanal* (figure 12). Both of these pictures evoke associations of Ariadne through their allusion to Dionysus. Yet neither Titian nor Rubens was painting Ariadne per se, but rather creating a scene of revelry and abandonment. What all these reclining figures have in common is the gesture of the arm over the head. This gesture always connotes sleep or, in some contexts, the Titian and the Rubens, for instance, an abandonment to sexual pleasure. The figure on the Portland vase is described by Erasmus Darwin as falling into the sleep of death, and in Cumberland's design the gesture clearly indicates a sleeping Cupid. Blake had therefore seen these two associations of the design – sleep and abandonment – before he came to use the figure in *J* 63, and in adding his own new detail, the worm wrapped about the figure, he added a powerful new dimension to the image.

The worm, for Blake and in literary tradition, connotes mortality. "I wish you joy of the worm," said Shakespeare's old man, delivering the asp to Cleopatra. Blake had wrapped a worm around Adam in his powerful colour print *Elohim Creating Adam*. Here, the combination of the worm and the female nude with its associations of Cleopatra, Ariadne, and Bacchanalia results in an image of the female principle very relevant to Blake's poetic text. Fritz Saxl has found classical models for nearly all the figures in Rubens's and Titian's paintings. He writes: "It is a remarkable fact that it is the greatest masters who turn to the great creations of the past and try to make them their own starting point. The works they produce are not copies – even if copies are intended, as in the case of Rubens ...[32] And we can be confident that Blake knew the associations his audience would bring to his illustrations for *J* 63. No one-to-one allegorical interpretation is possible, but a whole complex of associations can enrich the image.

In his own idiom, Blake was speaking the language of art. Its importance to him he summed up in his *Descriptive Catalogue*: "Milton, Shakspeare, Michael Angelo, Rafael, the finest specimens of Ancient Sculpture and Painting, and Architecture, Gothic, Grecian, Hindoo and Egyptian, are the extent of the human mind. The human mind cannot go beyond the gift of God, the Holy Ghost. To suppose that Art can go beyond the finest specimens of Art that are now in the world, is not knowing what Art is; it is being blind to the gifts of the spirit" (E 544).

NE

Blake's Metaphors of Form

"What kind of Intellects must he have who sees only the Colours of things & not the Forms of Things," exclaimed Blake with some exasperation in his "Public Address" (E 578). Seeing the "Forms of Things" was for Blake the key to imaginative life and the liberation of the spirit. Blake's concept of form infuses his poetry and painting, realizing itself in the linearity of his style as an artist and in his critical attitudes and aesthetic ideas. It is a dynamic concept, for it involves a relationship between the artist and his chosen media: the incising of a line on metal, the appearance of the image on paper. A word becomes a visual form when printed, while its power is undiminished and can produce of itself an image in the mind. In this chapter I will explore some of the implications of Blake's verbal and visual statements about form, principally examining his ideas concerning Eternal Form and Fallen Form. These ideas illuminate the purpose of the borrowed images we have been discussing.

In my opinion, Blake's ideas about form do not appear to have changed a great deal over the years. This is not to say that his aesthetic ideas did not alter at all, for his experiments with techniques and styles are by now well documented, but the basic principles of his aesthetic – his distinction between Eternal Form and Fallen Form, his insistence on the bounding lines – were constant, as was his lifelong, recurring use of certain visual symbols.

In this matter I disagree with Anne Kostelanetz Mellor, whose *Blake's Human Form Divine* argues for the presence of a changing conception of form in Blake's work and thus implies a basic contradiction in his theory and practice through much of his life.[1] In my view, Blake was *always* aware of the paradox that we are prisoners of form even though the line the artist draws upon chaos is his deliverance. Blake's solution was his conviction that the line must be made to work *for* man, as well as delineating his fallen form; hence his system of using the same visual image with either a regenerate or a fallen meaning, depending on the context of his writing.

Because Blake's concept of form is intricately connected to so much of his thinking and creative activity, I shall begin with an abbreviated account of the nature of form in Blake's writing, developing later various aspects of the topic.[2]

Form is one of Blake's most important words – over four pages in the *Concordance* are devoted to this one word, not counting the past tense of the verb – and though the word may take on philosophical implications of some complexity in his work, basically it always means for Blake what it did for Dr Johnson, "the External Appearance of Anything; representation; shape." Even when Blake uses *form* to mean the Platonic Idea, *eîdós* – that is, the permanent reality of a thing – the meaning of shape or image is always present:

> Whatever can be Created can be Annihilated Forms cannot
> The Oak is cut down by the Ax, the Lamb falls by the Knife
> But their Forms Eternal Exist, For-ever. (*M* 32: 36–8; E 132)

The matrix out of which all forms derive is the Real Man, or Poetic Genius (Blake's early term for imagination):

> Principle 1st. That the Poetic Genius is the true Man and that the body or outward form of Man is derived from the Poetic Genius ... which by the Ancients was calld an Angel & Spirit & Demon. (*ARO*, E 1)

When Blake thought of the creative faculty, imagination, he consistently did so in terms of the human body, "the Human Form Divine," which was also the image of God ("God becomes as we are, that we may be as he is"). These quotations from Blake's earliest illuminated tracts, *All Religions Are One* and *There Is No Natural Religion* (1788), are reiterated in annotations late in his career: "Imagination or the Human Eternal Body in Every Man ... The All in Man The Divine Image or Imagination" (*Siris* [annotations dated 1820], E 663). The equation of Human Body–Divine Image–Imagination is extended further by Blake's words on the *Laocoön* plate (1820):

> The Eternal Body of Man is The Imagination, that is God himself
> The Divine Body [Yeshua] Jesus We are his Members (E 273).

Jean Hagstrum writes of this inscription, "God is Christ, Christ is Imagination, Imagination is Man. One may put these noble nouns in any other order one chooses – the important fact remains that all are equal and each ends up becoming the other."[3]

The visual equivalent of this equation in Blake's art is the cruciform standing or "dancing" figure, which represents man at his extremes of potential: as Christ, Albion, or Los – and Satan (see figures 49, 63). It is not surprising that the human form itself, its outline and lineaments, meant so much to Blake, for the engraver and painter who is concerned with the visual form of things can only represent the human image as an outline of the human body, whether it is to represent the flesh *or* the spirit. The importance of the human form to Blake's art is further illumined by the realization that he is emphasizing that *all* forms we perceive are also *human*, that is, extensions of the human form, if we will only recognize them. The great final lines of *Jerusalem* assert: "All Human Forms identified even Tree Metal Earth & Stone ..." To anyone who perceives life in this way, the Newtonian universe holds no terrors.

It is essentially a Platonic myth that Blake offers as an antidote to a Newtonian world-view.[4] Blake's eventual strictures against the Greeks and "Mathematical Form" do not obviate the Platonic basis of his concepts. For Blake, the "Forms Eternal" exist in the imagination, which both creates and perceives them; Plato, of course, did not trust the imagination, and his hostility to the poetic experience is antipathetic to Blake. Yet, as Peter Fisher has written, "The aim of Plato is the aim of Blake: the Vision of what eternally exists; but the means are different."[5] With regard to the means, Blake writes: "All Forms are Perfect in the Poet's Mind, but these are not abstracted nor Compounded from Nature (but are from Imagination)" (*Annotations to Reynolds* [circa 1808], E 648).

Where Blake sharply diverges from Plato is in the idea that form and substance are separable. In this Blake is Aristotelian, declaring that "Man has no Body distinct from his Soul for that calld Body is a portion of Soul discernd by the five Senses. the chief inlets of Soul in this age" (*MHH*, E 34). George Mills Harper sees in this statement from *The Marriage* Blake contradicting himself,[6] but I hope to demonstrate that there is no contradiction. Blake, as ever, takes from both Plato and Aristotle what he needs to forge his own poetic and philosophical images.

Blake's essential difference with Plato is surely a disagreement with Plato's dualism: in Blake, Eternal Form and Fallen Form (or vegetative form) are essentially the same – they exist in one and the same body, and they exist *in the flesh*. It is not that there is a physical body *and* a spiritual body; they are rather two aspects of one:

> An outside shadowy Surface superadded to the real Surface;
> Which is unchangeable for ever & ever. (*J* 83: 47–8; E 242)[7]

This image implies a central core *inside* a Fallen Form or a shadowy cover over an Eternal Form. Blake's Milton calls the Spectre, the reasoning power in Man, a "false Body: an Incrustation over my Immortal Spirit" (*M* 40: 34–6; E 142). He goes on to speak of intending to "wash off the Not Human."

So the idea of the shadow as a *cover* develops in two ways: the shadow becomes a synonym for *spectre* (Enion weaves her own shadow, and views it in horror after having also woven Tharmas's Spectre in *The Four Zoas*, and the shadow image consolidates in the idea of the Covering Cherub, who is the ultimate personification of the Fallen Form.[8] In *Milton*, Blake catalogues all the false churches, or "Dragon Forms," and says, "All these are seen in Miltons Shadow who is the Covering Cherub / The Spectre of Albion ..." (*M* 37: 44; E 138). This idea, then, of the real or eternal hidden *within* a false covering is a basic concept for Blake and allows him to bridge the old philosophic dichotomy between flesh and spirit. It places the issue solely in the realm of perception, in the perceiving of a *form* which is mental rather than material. For the Newtonian world-view – the prevailing empirical or deistic spirit of the age – was the intellectual force that Blake believed he had to contend with. Like Bunyan and Spenser, Blake knew he must create an image for error in order that people might perceive it. The prime emblematic image of Fallen Form is the Covering Cherub or Antichrist, just as the main emblematic image of Eternal Form is Jesus.

Blake often expresses these ideas in the lexis of clothing. "Luvah's robes of blood" are Blake's symbol of the Incarnation and, as Morton Paley has written,[9] are likely to suggest the robes in which Jesus was clothed when he was mocked and beaten (Matt. 27:28), thus emphasizing the meaning of mortality attached to them. Paley has examined the importance of garments and weaving symbols in detail in *The Four Zoas*, *Milton*, and *Jerusalem*. He has brought together all important references to the garment image, and he also points to its importance in Blake's designs.

Paley, like Harper, believes that Blake's attitude to the body was ambivalent – that is, that there is a contradiction inherent in saying "Man has no Body distinct from his Soul" and at the same time suggesting in *Visions of the Daughters of Albion* or *Europe* that we are trapped in our bodies. Paley argues that Blake uses the image of the garment as an ambiguous symbol which allows him a way out of the contradiction: it is *both* a fallen and a "resurrected" symbol:

> Los said to Enitharmon Pitying I saw
> Pitying the Lamb of God Descended thro Jerusalems gates
> To put off Mystery time after time & as a Man
> Is born on Earth so was he born of Fair Jerusalem
> In mysterys woven mantle & in the Robes of Luvah
>
> He stood in fair Jerusalem to awake up into Eden
> The fallen Man but first to Give his vegetated body
> To be cut off & separated that the Spiritual body may be Reveald
>
> (*FZ* VIII: 104; E 378).

Paley writes:

> In this simultaneous double perspective, the body-garment is perceived as constituting at one and the same time the entrapping and the redemptive aspects

13 Blake, illustration to Edward Young's *Night Thoughts* 114

(5)

But grant to Life (and juſt it is to grant
To *lucky* Life) ſome Perquiſites of Joy;
A Time there is, when like a thrice-told Tale,
And that of no great Moment, or Delight,
Long-rifled Life of Sweet can yeild no more,
But from our *Comment* on the Comedy,
Pleaſing *Reflections* on Parts well-ſuſtain'd,
Or purpos'd *Emendations* where we fail'd,
Or Hopes of Plaudits from our candid Judge,
When, on their Exit, Souls are bid unrobe,
Toſs *Fortune* back her Tinſel, and her Plume,
And drop this Maſk of Fleſh behind the Scene.

With me, that Time is come; my World is dead;
A new World riſes, and new Manners reign:
Foreign Comedians, a ſpruce Band! arrive,
To puſh me from the Scene, or hiſs me there.
What a pert Race ſtars up? the Strangers gaze,
And I at them; my Neighbour is unknown;
Nor that the worſt; ah me! the dire Effect

which have hitherto been seen as opposed alternatives. Furthermore, a new ambiguity is introduced. If the vegetated body is a garment which is finally to be "cut off," what is the spiritual body but another kind of garment?[10]

Here I do not agree with Paley that the spiritual body may be seen also *as* a garment. I think it important to notice that it is "revealed" and not donned. It is already there, underneath. It is the essence. It cannot be stripped away. There is a design by Blake for Night IV of Edward Young's *Night Thoughts* (*NT* 114; see figure 13) illustrating the lines:

Toss *Fortune* back her Tinsel and her Plume
And drop this Mark of Flesh behind the Scene.

The design shows a female figure dropping a mask, shoes, and filmy garment. The naked figure is left. This is not to say that the spiritual body may not *wear* a garment; as Paley brilliantly demonstrates, Blake's technique suggests garments and nakedness simultaneously:

In *The Soul hovering over the Body reluctantly parting with Life*, the male corpse wears a shroud that obscures the lines of his body while the female soul wears a filmy high-waisted gown that would have been quite modish at a Regency ball; and in *The meeting of a Family in Heaven* all the figures are clothed in garments whose drapery reveals rather than conceals the contours of the human body. In *The Day of Judgment* some of the rising blessed are similarly clothed while others are naked, showing that in these *Grave* pictures, as in *Jerusalem*, Blake does not conceive of the risen body as either necessarily naked or necessarily clothed. The male figure in *The Reunion of the Soul and the Body* even wears a trailing skirtlike garment similar to that pictured in *Jerusalem* 95 (35), while the descending female's gown unfurling behind her echoes this motif. What is particularly impressive about the three pictures just referred to is the erotic nature of the embraces, whether the figures are clothed as the husband and wife meeting in heaven or naked as the couple at the lower left in *The Day of Judgment*. One feels that these figures are well on their way to comminglings from head to foot. Nor is the ambiguity of the Blakean body-garment an invention of our twentieth-century consciousness. Coleridge, in commenting on the Songs, complained about "the ambiguity of the Drapery" in the title-page illustration. "Is it a garment," he asked, "or the body incised and scored out?" The answer is of course either, or both, for close-fitting, filmy clothing suggestive of being the body itself was already characteristic of Blake's pictorial vocabulary by 1789.[11]

In my opinion, it is the transient nature of the mortal garment which both Blake's poetry and his designs of the human form emphasize. His designs suggest garments and nakedness simultaneously, and his drawing of translucent garments is intended to suggest the Eternal Form underneath. His poetry reaffirms the analogy between the clothing symbol and the shadowy cover which obscures Eternal Form. At the end of a long passage in *Milton* 41, about casting off falsehood and rationality, "the rotten rags of memory," Blake sums up:

> These are the destroyers of Jerusalem, these are the murderers
> of Jesus ...
> These are the Sexual Garments, the Abomination of Desolation
> Hiding the Human Lineaments as with an Ark & Curtains
> Which Jesus rent ... (*M* 41: 21–7; E 142)

Again, the human lineaments, in their Eternal Form, are there underneath, waiting to be revealed. Similarly, in *The Four Zoas*:

> He stood in fair Jerusalem to awake up into Eden
> The fallen Man but first to Give his vegetated body
> To be cut off & separated that the Spiritual body may be Reveald
> (*FZ* VIII: 104; E 378).

The mortal body is cut away like a garment.

The location of the Eternal Form is always *within* or *inside*, and of course this directional symbolism is a familiar part of Blakean language:

> ... in your own Bosom you bear your Heaven
> And Earth, & all you behold, tho it appears Without it is Within
> In your Imagination of which this World of Mortality is but a Shadow.
> (*J* 71: 17–19; E 225)

When the Eternal Form does wear a garment, the "material" will be *light*, the opposite of shadow:

> In Great Eternity, every particular Form gives forth or Emanates
> Its own peculiar Light, & the Form is the Divine Vision
> And the Light is his Garment (*J* 54: 1–3; E 203).

To summarize at this point what we have seen to be the qualities of Eternal Form: it is human-shaped; it is within, covered as it were by a selfish exterior which is as a shadow covering the real substance; it is translucent. There is another significant quality to Eternal Form as Blake conceived it, and that is *energy*. Eternal forms are constantly in motion:

> ... and they [the human forms] walked
> To & Fro in Eternity as One Man reflecting each in each & clearly seen
> And seeing: according to fitness & order. (*J* 98: 38–40; E 258)

Movement and energy are, of course, an important quality of Blake's visual art, and the concept has been investigated by various scholars, notably Morton Paley and E.J. Rose. In Blake's eternity, creative energies may change, though their essential forms do not. I interpret the passage above to mean that the images of man through the ages can have various contexts (such as painting, literature, music, architecture, or science) while still retaining their eternal human image ("such was the variation of Time and Space / Which vary according as the Organs of Perception vary").

A final quality to note about Blake's idea of Eternal Form is that, though forms reflect each other, merging and exchanging light, they do not lose their individual identities. Blake is very clear on what identity means: he uses the word *identity* to mean *particularized form* or individuality. The link between identity and form runs through his writings:

> In Eternity one Thing never Changes into another Thing
> Each Identity is Eternal ... (*VLJ*, E 556)

> The Infinite alone resides in Definite Determinate Identity
> (*J* 55: 64; E 205).

> All Human Forms identified ... (*J* 99: 1; E 258)

> They are all firm, determinate outline, or identical form. (Remarks on the drawings of Thomas Heath Malkin from *A Father's Memoirs of his Child* by Benjamin Heath Malkin, E 693)

Indeed, when Blake refers on two occasions to a state "Beyond the Outline of Identity" (*M* 37: 10; *J* 18: 3), he means chaos or nonentity, the opposite of form.

Thus, an essential quality of Eternal Form is extreme clarity of outline. Blake writes:

> The Man who asserts that there is no Such Thing as Softness in Art & that every thing in Art is Definite & Determinate has not been told this by Practise but by Inspiration & Vision because Vision is Determinate & Perfect & he Copies that without Fatigue (*Annotations to Reynolds*, E 646).

The "distinct, sharp and wirey" bounding line is therefore an integral part of Eternal Forms in the pictorial arts: "leave out this line and you leave out life itself; all is chaos again ..." (*A Descriptive Catalogue*, E 550). Anything formless or indefinite, then, like clouds or water, or even art which is soft in outline, like the work of Rembrandt or Rubens, becomes images of the fallen, not the eternal world. That is why, in Generation (Blake's late term for the world of Experience), the forms themselves can change, as in "The Crystal Cabinet" or "The Mental Traveller," or Tirzah becoming Rahab. This aspect of the Two-fold Vision can be seen in some designs where Blake uses a kind of visual pun as a means of ironic comment. Designs which show a form changing can be found in *America* 16, where the hair of the kneeling figure becomes a waterfall, or in *M* 19, where Los turns into a tree. In *Jerusalem*, where this device is used seriously and frequently, we can find a swan becoming human (*J* 11), a female figure turning to roots (*J* 74), and Los's entrails becoming grapevines (*J* 85). In Eternity one thing may never change into another thing, but in the fallen world they do.

It is essential to the understanding of Blake's aesthetic to realize the differences between Eternal Form and Fallen Form, yet the paradox must always be recognized that they are essentially the same – it is only our perception of them that differs. Fallen perception projects Fallen Form – "As a man is, so he sees." Thomas Frosch's study *The Awakening of Albion: The Renovation of the Body in the Poetry of William Blake* brilliantly elucidates this, showing anew that renewal for Blake is not a transcendence but a reorganization of the given.[12] Man's body, the archetypal form, is the result of the desires of all Blakean characters, who fear nonentity more than anything else: the instinct for form is one of their basic drives. One reason for this is that the human form is proof of the existence of imagination: "the body or outward form of Man is derived from the Poetic Genius," as Blake wrote in *All Religions Are One*.

But the body, or "outward form of man," presented certain problems to Blake, as it had to thinkers before him. St Paul describes two bodies, a natural one and a spiritual one.[13] Aquinas had distinguished a spiritual world with "subsistent forms" (*formae separatae*) from the material world with its "inherent forms," which exist only in combination with matter. Blake, too, had to distinguish between these two aspects of form, but his task was complicated not only because he was attempting to draw them for us as well as express the ideas in poetry, but because he conceived Fallen Form and Eternal Form as basically the same, and existing in the flesh. Thus his descriptions of Fallen Form, and the creation of it, are horrific, for he describes the warping and disfigurement of an ideal form, the human body. These accounts occur principally in *The Book of Urizen*, the Books of *Los* and *Ahania*, and *The Four Zoas*, where they describe the creation of the body of Urizen.

To appreciate fully what is happening in these accounts, we must realize that they are concerned first of all with the horror of *formlessness*. The Fall has meant a disintegration of human faculties, a fall out of unity and order and therefore out of form, and Blake tells the story both as the creation of Urizen and also as the fall of Tharmas. But since Tharmas does not appear in Blake's poetry until *The Four Zoas* (circa 1797), it is useful to look first at *Urizen*.

To begin with, Urizen has no body, and is described as "a shadow of horror," an "abominable void," a "soul-shudd'ring vacuum" (*BU* 3: 1–5; E 70). As his separation and division continue, Urizen gradually turns into unformed *matter*: "The petrific abominable chaos" (*BU* 3: 26; E 71).[14] Urizen is "Unorganiz'd, rent from Eternity," and is recognized by the

Eternals as "Death," "a clod of clay" (*BU* 6: 11; E 74). Los, the fallen imagination, frightened by "the formless, unmeasurable death," has thrown a net about and "bound every change" of Urizen. The word *bound* means here not primarily "tying down" but rather the meaning given first place in Johnson's *Dictionary*, of being a limit or a boundary. In this way Blake allegorizes the methods of the psyche trying to save itself: it must give form to its environment. In the *Book of Los*, Blake further describes the process as "incessant the falling Mind labour'd / Organizing itself: till the Vacuum / Became element ..." (E 92).

In this account of the Fall, from Los's point of view, Los first destroys the stony chaos of the unformed Urizen but, in doing so, falls into the void himself. As he strives to organize his environment, he also achieves a fallen body of sorts, "an immense Fibrous form," the Polypus (which becomes another of Blake's symbols of fallen nature). But Los at least is able to organize his body finally in order to give form to Urizen:

> Upfolding his Fibres together
> To a Form of impregnable strength
> Los astonish'd and terrified, built
> Furnaces; he formed an Anvil
> A Hammer of adamant then began
> The binding of Urizen day and night (*BU* 4: 18–24; E 94).

But of course, all of Los's titanic efforts to give form to the vacuum only result in *fallen* form:

> ... till a Form
> Was completed, a Human Illusion
> In darkness and deep clouds involvd. (*BU* 4: 54–6; E 94)

We may note the details of the fallen body of Urizen: Blake describes first the circular motion of the "bounded" mind, rolling "Eddies of wrath ceaseless round and round" till its final shape is an orb, "his fountain of thought" (E 75). This circular image becomes a hallmark both of Urizenic thought processes and of Urizenic design. Then follows the formation of skeleton, eyes, ears, nose, stomach and throat, arms and legs, in seven ages – all described in terms of woe, torment, and anguish. (The seven ages, an ironic reminder of the seven days of Creation, suggest that Urizen's body is analogous to the fallen world.) Thus cut off from his eternal body, the self-enclosed nature of Urizen's fallen form is drawn by Blake consistently in circular, huddled shapes. These shapes I have called despair figures (in chapter 4), for Blake used them all his life with this meaning, but they are particularly evident in the Lambeth books. In *The Book of Urizen*, the shapes are as grotesque as any he ever draws, and torment and anguish are evident in their expressions. In the colour print *Elohim Creating Adam*, like *The Book of Urizen* a product of

1795, the expressions of anguish as man is created in the image of his god are often remarked. In this design, however, a hint of the fallen divinity of the human form remains in the cruciform attitudes of both figures.

The achievement of Fallen Form is a terrible thing, then, but it is at least better than nothingness, than the void which the fall from Eternal Form threatens. Blake appears to have given this matter further consideration by the time he expanded his account of the Fall in *The Four Zoas*, for here he sets the action explicitly in the human psyche and begins not with the fall of Urizen but with the fall of Tharmas.

It is by now a cliché of Blake criticism to call Tharmas the symbol of bodily sensation: what is not so often made explicit is that bodily sensation is the body's sense of its own form. This ability is necessary for the Eternal Man, who, even though mingling with other forms, is always aware of his own identity. Another way of expressing this is to say that Tharmas is the faculty which perceives order. This faculty in the Eternal Man keeps all parts of the human image functioning harmoniously and is not limited to the five fallen senses: "Mans perceptions are not bounded by organs of perception he percieves more than sense (tho' ever so acute) can discover" (*TNR* b 1; E 2).

The "Parent Power" which holds the Eternal Man together is thus not only energy of sensation but an aesthetic force as well. This idea may best be demonstrated by noting Tharmas's connection with poetry in eternity and his friendly relationship there with Urthona, the artist (*FZ* IX: 137; E 405). Both are engaged with form and aesthetic shape. When Tharmas falls, the sense of order becomes fallen as well, and the first image lost is the form of one's environment – in Blake's terms, one's Emanation. Tharmas's first words are "Lost! Lost! Lost! are my Emanations Enion O Enion."

From Tharmas's plight, something of the nature of the Emanation becomes apparent. When he can no longer perceive his Emanation, he is in danger of formlessness. He knows how necessary Enion is:

> I am almost Extinct & soon shall be a Shadow in Oblivion
> Unless some way can be found that I may look upon thee & live
> (*FZ* I: 4; E 301).

> ... I am like an atom
> A Nothing left in darkness yet I am an identity
> I wish & feel & weep & groan Ah terrible terrible (*FZ* I: 4; E 302).

Thereafter, Tharmas sinks "down into the sea a pale white corse." His Spectre or Fallen Form eventually emerges, drawn out by his Emanation in the "loom of Vegetation" that is nature. Like the fallen form of Urizen, the fallen form of Tharmas is called Death (E 303). Blake gives the Spectre of Tharmas a beautiful image: a human form fallen, yet with a visible potential for Eternal Form:

> ... soon in masculine strength augmenting he
> Reard up a form of gold & stood upon the glittering rock
> A shadowy human form winged (*FZ* I: 6; E 303).

This new form of Tharmas is like Lucifer:

> ... & in his depths
> The dazzlings as of gems shone clear, rapturous in fury
> Glorying in his own eyes Exalted in Terrific Pride (E 303).

Indeed, in *Jerusalem* he will become for Blake the Covering Cherub or Satan, the epitome of Fallen Form.

In this shape, Tharmas knows Enion and mates with her,[15] and she gives birth to Los and Enitharmon, who becomes symbolic of time and space. In other words, Fallen Form (Spectre of Tharmas) and its offspring are the world as we know it. Blake has defined this in many ways in his work, from Los creating a form for Urizen, as we have seen, to, later, Milton "forming bright Urizen" (E 114), but early and later the message remains the same: Nature is the realization or embodiment of Fallen Form and simultaneously the outline of the Eternal Form which resides within it.

The earliest of Blake's works to consider the distinctions between the Eternal Form and the Fallen is *The Book of Thel* (engraved 1789). I believe that Thel is a maiden of Innocence and a real person, as Anne Kostelanetz Mellor, Nancy Bogen, and others argue. But also, in my view, she is an Eternal Form, whose perceptions are so heightened that she can speak to the Lilly, the Cloud, the Clod of Clay. Like the Eternal Forms that Blake would later describe in *Jerusalem* giving forth their own "peculiar Light" (*J* 54: 1–2), Thel is described in terms of shimmering light and radiance: she is associated with morning beauty, a "watry" bow, a parting cloud, a reflection, shadows in water, dreams, smiles, and music, and called a "shining woman." She laments that she is insubstantial, as this lucidity appears to her to be a kind of transient formlessness: "I pass away: yet I complain."[16]

However, the other "characters" of the poem (except the Worm and the Clod of Clay, who are of the state of Experience) are described in terms of similar lucidity: the Lilly describes herself as "clothed in light" every morning (*Thel* I: 23; E 4); the Cloud is a "bright form," hovering and glittering in the air. These inhabitants of the Vale of Har are also Eternal Forms, who, unlike Thel, realize that their "mortality" does not deprive them of external existence. As the Cloud says, "O maid I tell thee, when I pass away It is to tenfold life ..." (II: 10; E 4)

The Clod of Clay, mother of the Worm, can offer Thel another mode of existence. Thel wants to be of use in the world, and the fallen world could benefit from her service; yet when Thel is given the opportunity of form in Experience, a fallen body with its enclosed senses (ears, eyes, tongue, nostrils, sex), she is frightened away. (The House of Clay need not detain her, for as an Eternal Form it is given to her to enter and return at will.) Thel in effect refuses Fallen Form.

Leaving for a moment the implications of Thel's refusal, there are obviously described in this poem two states of existence, an eternal and a generative or fallen state, both existing *within* nature. The illustrations of the poem bear out this idea, for in almost every case they portray a kind of double perspective or personification of nature, as when, on the title-page, Thel sees the lovers emerging from flowers, on plate 2 the Lilly is seen as a woman, and on plate 4 the Cloud as a man and the Worm an infant. In this manner the essential human form of the natural world is illuminated.

Was Thel's refusal of Fallen Form mistaken or was it justified? Much of the critical controversy that has surrounded this poem has centred on the final plate (which Blake is considered to have added after 1791, at the same time as Thel's Motto). Thel's action is commendable or not, depending upon what her original state is taken to be. If Thel is considered to be a spirit who refuses embodiment, then her act is commendable if the critic is – or thinks Blake is – anti-materialist. Thel is mistaken if the critic thinks that all souls must pass through the world of Experience. If Thel is considered a human being, then her refusal means a refusal of maturity and sexual awakening, and is therefore misguided. Anne Mellor argues that Thel, a real woman, belongs to a world of Innocence which must consciously preserve itself against self-repression (*Blake's Human Form Divine*, page 20). Thel's refusal of Experience is justified: "Thel neither can nor should tolerate the evil and unnatural repressions of this 'land of sorrows'" (page 34). Mellor feels also that Blake changed his mind about the virtues of Experience circa 1791 and that Thel's refusal reflects a change of heart towards the human form. She suggests that the original (1789) ending to *Thel* would have had Thel enter her grave plot (that is, experience sexual union and motherhood) and then return to Har at peace with herself and life. This is an interesting idea, and one way of accounting for the illustrations of plate 6, but it does not make for a very dramatic poem and furthermore supposes a technical change to the plate (re-engraving) which cannot be established. However, if Thel is an Eternal Form – a state of existence all human beings are capable of achieving in Blake's view – her refusal to become a Fallen Form is justified. Blake may have added this plate later, but I too would argue that his original intention was always to have Thel refuse the Fallen Form of her eternal body.

And yet we do feel an uneasiness at the conclusion of *Thel*. If Eternal Form refuses to enter into Fallen Form, the fallen cannot be redeemed. Thel *should* be able to perceive "more than sense ... can discover" (*TNR* 6 1). Is there perhaps another way of looking at the final plate of *Thel*? She does, after all, enter her grave-plot willingly, expecting to be "cherished with milk and oil" by Mother Earth as the Worm was. But the voice that she hears rejects every single liberated sense that her Eternal Form brings with it.

Is it so surprising that she flees? She is not yet ready to accept her form in the fallen world. She has been given permission to enter and return, and she chooses to return. Hers is a failure of perception, an immaturity of spirit. She cannot see the hidden Eternal Form of the fallen world.

TWO

The Visual Languages of the Passions

William Blake lived in a world of human images, as we all do, but he had a rare compulsion to understand them. It was not only that he considered their symbolic meanings in art but that he scrutinized the very conformation of the human face and figure, its expressions, attitudes, and gestures, and codified them into a personal visual language. Theorists of painting call this a study of the Passions, and it was not an unusual study for artists of the late seventeenth and eighteenth centuries; what is unusual is the individual use Blake made of it in much of his art and the manner in which he continued to rely on his visual language as a kind of shorthand.

"Passion and Expression is Beauty Itself – The Face that is Incapable of Passion & Expression is Deformity Itself," Blake wrote in one of his *Annotations to Reynolds* (E 653). The words *passion* and *expression* meant something different to Blake and his contemporaries from what they mean to us, for they brought with them associations of a set of conventions which governed the portrayal of emotions in all the arts.[1] The long tradition of the doctrine of the Passions – "the sturdiest branch of the withering tree of faculty psychology"[2] – which goes back to Aristotle and beyond, was in full flower in the early eighteenth century and has all but disappeared today. For Blake, the study of the language of gesture would have been both necessary and natural to his early training in Henry Pars's drawing school, and the most famous treatises of theory of gesture were surely familiar to him. Here we will survey some of the visual languages available to Blake in tracts and manuals produced over the previous 150 years for the artist, for the actor, and for the dancer. The language of art is the language of the Passions cast in familiar types and attitudes, and to become familiar with this language was the aim of every student. It was a language of facial expressions, of hand and body gestures, and of pantomimic attitudes: in this chapter we will relate each category in turn to examples of Blake's work.

A drawing school's method of imparting this language was to set the student to copying – both from live models and from outlines drawn in copy-books. "To learn the Language of Art, Copy Forever is My Rule," Blake wrote in his *Annotations to Reynolds*. It is notable that though Blake is usually vociferously opposed to Reynolds's opinions in *The Discourses*, when Reynolds approves of copying, Blake is in complete agreement. When Reynolds writes, "[Nice copying teaches] exactness and precision ...," Blake responds, "Excellent" (E 644). When Reynolds subordinates copying to amassing a stock of ideas, or "laying up materials," Blake exclaims, "What is Laying up materials but Copying" (E 644). And when Reynolds suggests that "the great use in copying, if it be at all useful, should seem to be in learning to colour ...," Blake writes, "*Contemptible*."[3]

As we have seen in our discussion of his treatment of form, Blake saw no contradiction between copying and creating. For him, to copy the attitudes previous generations had used in their painting was to participate in the language of art. The individual artist's vision enabled him to produce a transformation of an inherited attitude, and for Blake this was the copying of imagination. He disapproved of imitation, which he equated with memory. He also made great claims for his own originality – "I know my Execution is not like Any Body Else I do not intend it to be so (none but Blockheads copy one another)" ("Public Address," E 582). But it is clear that he learned his trade and laid up his materials, like many other artists, under the tutelage of drawing books and the tracts of Charles LeBrun, Gerard de Lairesse, and Johann Caspar Lavater.

Charles LeBrun (1619–90) dominated the artistic world of seventeenth-century France; he was the foremost painter of the Gobelins factory and the furnishings director of Versailles, the creator of the style of Louis XIV. LeBrun's famous essay, *Expression des Passions* (1698) was published first in English in 1701 by the London firm of John Smith, Edward Cooper, and David Mortimer, appearing also in Dutch, French, and Italian editions. The English title was *A Method to Learn to Design the Passions*, and it was widely read throughout the eighteenth century, commented upon by Hogarth, Reynolds, Richardson, and Fuseli. The edition familiar to Blake would have probably been John Williams's translation of 1734.

LeBrun's essay concentrates directly on facial expressions, with outline illustrations of these. He includes a few notes on bodily attitudes, such as: "Ravishment or Extasy may represent the Body cast downwards, the Arms lifted up, and the Hands open; the whole Action expressing a transport of Joy."[4] This may remind Blake's readers of the illustrations in *Milton*, showing William and Robert receiving the spirit of Milton (see figures 58 and 59).

The longer and more detailed work of Gerard de Lairesse (1641–1711) exerted an almost equal influence on the age. In his essay published in Amsterdam in 1707 and translated into English in 1738 as *The*

Art of Painting in All Its Branches, Lairesse directs much attention to techniques of colouring and describing the drawing of bodily gestures. Although Lairesse's brief illustrations of gesture and stance do not appear to me to have influenced Blake, some passages advising artists how to make their meaning easily interpreted were probably part of the general lore that all art students learned. For instance, Lairesse advises, "To each Figure join its Mark of Distinction, to show what it is; as, whether a *King*, *Philosopher*, *Bacchus*, or *River God* ... The Philosopher is to be known by a *long and grave Vestment*, *Cap on his Head*, *Books*, *Rolls of Vellum*, and other *Implements of Study* about him."[5]

Lairesse's "Introduction to Drawing" from another work, *The Principles of Design*, was translated and included in a drawing manual published in England in 1751 under the name of "the late Mr. Lens, Miniature-Painter and Drawing Master to Christ's-Hospital." It contains much advice on clear outlines and copying methods and makes a useful comparison with the sketch-book of Robert Blake,[6] which William is believed to have directed. Lens's book is called *For the Curious Young Gentlemen and Ladies, that study and practise the noble and commendable Art of Drawing, Colouring and Japanning, a New and Compleat* DRAWING-BOOK; *Consisting of Variety of Classes, viz. Whole Figures in divers Positions, and all the several Parts of the Human Body from Head to Foot; light, airy, loose Landskips; Perspective Views of Sea-Ports, Forts, Ruins, etc* ...[7] The title reflects the age's interest in categories or classes as an aid to learning. The study of art was made as systematic as possible: it too was an exercise of reason. Drawing manuals like Lens's advocated the repeated drawing of "Parts of human Figures, as the Eye, the Ear, the Hand, Feet, etc." We see that this was the method William established for young Robert, who drew repeatedly eyes or legs from the example on the page by William.

Blake did not consider this "The Art of Painting" – "No Man of Sense can think that an Imitation of the Objects of Nature is The Art of Painting or that such Imitation which any one may easily perform is worthy of Notice ..."[8] – but it was none the less the laying up of materials, and he set his brother to it.

> I intreat then that the Spectator will attend to the Hands & Feet to the Lineaments of the Countenances they are all descriptive of character & not a line is drawn without intention & that most discriminate and particular. (*VLJ*, E 560)

This oft-quoted sentence from Blake's *Vision of the Last Judgment* will be given new contexts by the material which follows. The words reiterate Blake's absorption of the work by LeBrun and later of Johann Caspar Lavater's *Essays on Physiognomy*; they reflect his familiarity with an oratorial tradition going back to the seventeenth century and to the popular traditions of dramatic gesture and pantomime. The codifying of meaning of facial expression and gesture was a preoccupation of seventeenth and eighteenth-century men of letters, and Blake and his contemporaries employed their repeated motifs and attitudes fully conscious of those traditions.

THE LANGUAGE OF THE FACE

LeBrun's essay attempts to set out a vocabulary of expressions defining particular emotions. His theory is Cartesian, regularly emphasizing the relation between psychology and physiology.[9] LeBrun virtually put Descartes's psychology "on the tip of the young painters' brushes."[10] He mentions eleven passions which the ancient philosophers described in two categories, "the simple Passions in the concupiscible appetite, the fiercer and compound Passions in the irascible" (*Method*, page 15). Love, Hatred, Desire, Joy, and Sadness belong to the "concupiscible" category, while the "irascible" are Fear, Boldness, Hope, Despair, Anger, and Fright.[11] He writes:

> Others add the Passion of Admiration, which they place first; afterwards Love, Hatred, Desire, Joy and Sadness; and from these they derive such as are compounded, as Fear, Boldness, Hope, etc. (page 15)

After briefly discussing the physiology of these emotions as they are discernible in the pulse of breathing and other motions of the body, LeBrun concludes that "the Face is the Part of the Body where the Passions more particularly discover themselves" (page 20) and "the Eyebrow is the only Part of the whole face, where the Passions best make themselves known; tho' many will have it to be in the Eyes" (page 21). LeBrun had a powerful influence on Hogarth's painting of the face of the actor David Garrick as Richard III, and equally on acting technique itself.[12] LeBrun's instructions to painters are translatable into theatrical direction: for example, the description of Horror:

> the Eye-brow will be still more knit ... the Pupil, instead of appearing situate in the middle of the Eye, will be sunk low; the mouth will be half open, but more compressed in the middle than at the corners, which will seem drawn back ... (page 30)

The codification of the language of expression and the concomitant codifying of the emotions which is implied is surely behind three brief but powerful poems of Blake's, "The Divine Image," "A Divine Image," and "The Human Abstract." In these poems, Blake's "Passions" are Mercy, Pity, Peace, Love, Cruelty, Jealousy, Terror, Secrecy, Humility, and Deceit. Yet it is significant that it is the human *form* rather than the human *face* that Blake imagines as the true image of the divine: this is an important difference in emphasis from LeBrun's and must be kept in mind as we explore Blake's use of facial expressions. Blake's vision was so expansive that physiognomy alone was not expressive enough: it is not as a painter of the human face that we admire Blake. Nevertheless we can detect Blake following LeBrun in many cases, especially when he wishes to portray violent emotions.

14 Blake, *The Conversion of Saul*

A good example of a Blake picture in which LeBrun's system is discernible is the watercolour *Conversion of Saul* (see figure 14). The biblical text that Blake is illustrating is Acts 9:3–7, the account of Saul, the persecutor of Christians, confronted by a vision of Christ:

3 And as he journeyed, he came near Damascus: and suddenly there shined round about him a light from heaven:
4 And he fell to earth, and heard a voice saying unto him, Saul, Saul, why persecutest thou me?
5 And he said, who art thou, Lord? And the Lord said, I am Jesus whom thou persecutest: it is hard for thee to kick against the pricks.
6 And he trembling and astonished said, Lord, what wilt thou have me to do? And the Lord said unto him, Arise, and go into the city, and it shall be told thee what thou must do.
7 And the men which journeyed with him stood speechless, hearing a voice, but seeing no man.

Blake does not show Saul on the ground, as the text states. Instead, Saul receives the vision astride his horse, his body inclined slightly backwards and his arms outstretched in a cruciform gesture which both suggests and mirrors the divinity to which he is witness.[13]

Perhaps taking his cue from the biblical text, which describes Saul as "astonished," Blake has followed LeBrun's diagram of Astonishment (*L'Etonnement*; see figure 15), turning to profile, of course. However, the open mouth and wide-open eye are clearly marked. The resemblance of

15 LeBrun, *A Method to Learn to Design the Passions: Tranquillity, Astonishment, Admiration*

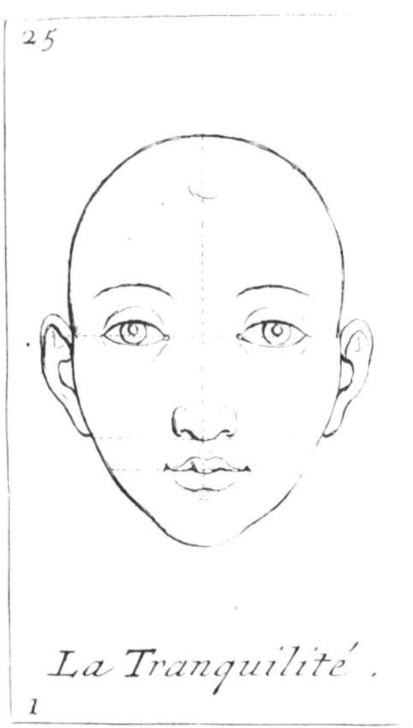

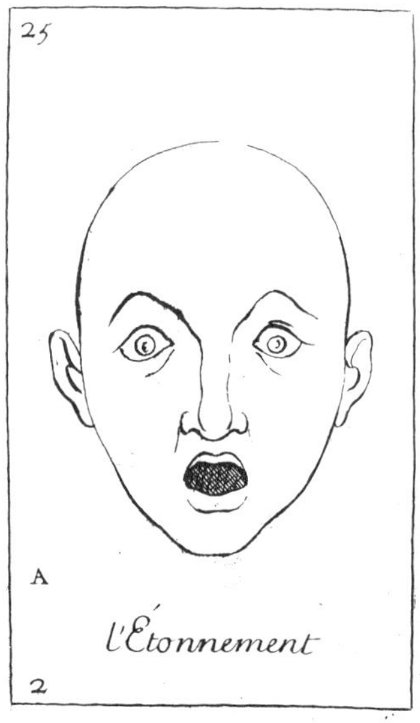

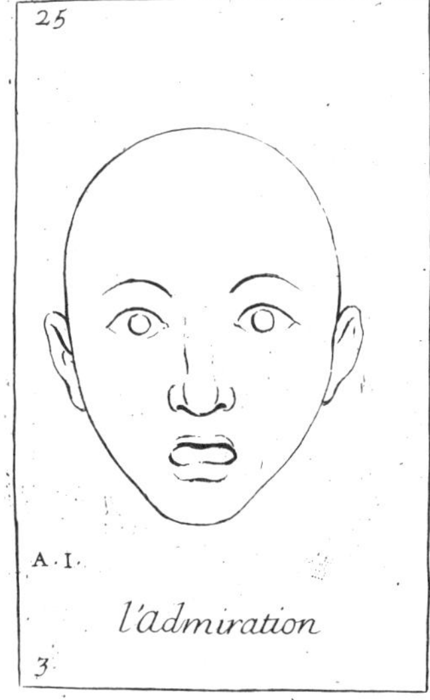

16 Blake, *The Great Red Dragon and the Woman Clothed with the Sun*

Saul's body position to LeBrun's description of Ravishment or Ecstasy recalls the designs of William and Robert receiving the spirit of Milton. (In addition, we may find a similar facial expression in profile on the woman in Blake's watercolour *The Great Red Dragon and the Woman Clothed with the Sun* [see figure 16], where her astonishment is certainly justified.) On the other hand, the expression of Christ in Saul's vision seems to be that of LeBrun's Tranquillity (*La Tranquilité*), with its closed mouth and curved brows (see figure 15). Because of Christ's raised arm and pointing finger, the moment illustrated is clearly verse 6, where Jesus says to the "astonished" Saul, "Arise and go into the city ..."[14]

Another of Blake's designs to show the influence of LeBrun is the colour print *Elohim Creating Adam* (figure 17). The similarity of the faces of Elohim and Adam to each other has been noticed; what has not been remarked is that the facial expressions conform to LeBrun's models for Bodily Pain (figure 18). One could even suggest that Elohim resembles LeBrun's Acute Pain (*Douleur Egüe*) and Adam the Extreme Bodily Pain

17 Blake, *Elohim Creating Adam*

18 LeBrun, *A Method to Learn to Design the Passions: Extreme Bodily Pain, Acute Pain*

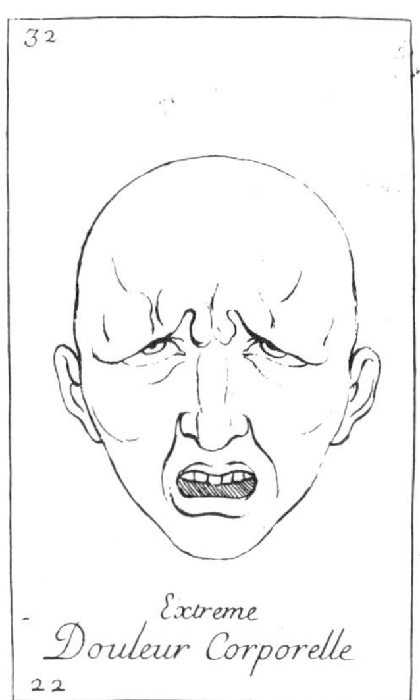

19 Blake, *Nebuchadnezzar*

(*Extrême Douleur Corporelle*) of the diagram.

Blake's colour print *Nebuchadnezzar* (see figure 19) also depicts a moment of extreme emotion as the king turns into a beast, and Blake may be seen here to have adopted LeBrun's Astonishment with Fright (*Étonnement avec frayeur*) and Horror (*L'horreur*) (see figure 20). Of Fright, LeBrun writes, "the Eyes must look wide open, the Upper-Eye-Lid be hid under the Brow, the White of the Eye surrounded with red, the Pupil appear wild, and situate more to the bottom of the Eye than upwards ..." (*Method*, page 31). In all this Blake follows, though Nebuchadnezzar's eyebrows are not raised in the middle, as LeBrun advocates, but rather have almost become part of his forehead. This emphasizes Nebuchadnezzar's bestial look.

Bo Lindberg has detected Blake using LeBrun's model of Contempt for Eliphaz in *Job* 12,[15] and it is true that one can detect LeBrun's formulae occasionally in *Job*, though in my opinion Blake depends there much more on gesture and bodily attitude to express meaning and emotion. Blake learned the language of art, the codifications and systems of expression and gesture, and then adapted them or developed some of his own formula figures. Yet since he rarely drew from live models, the store of images in his mind was no doubt reinforced by observing the repeatedly borrowed motifs of his contemporaries.[16]

Blake's acceptance of LeBrun was no doubt reinforced by his acquaintance with Lavater's widely read *Essays on Physiognomy*, for which he engraved four plates for the first volume of the English edition of 1789.

20 LeBrun, *A Method to Learn to Design the Passions: Horror, Astonishment with Fright*

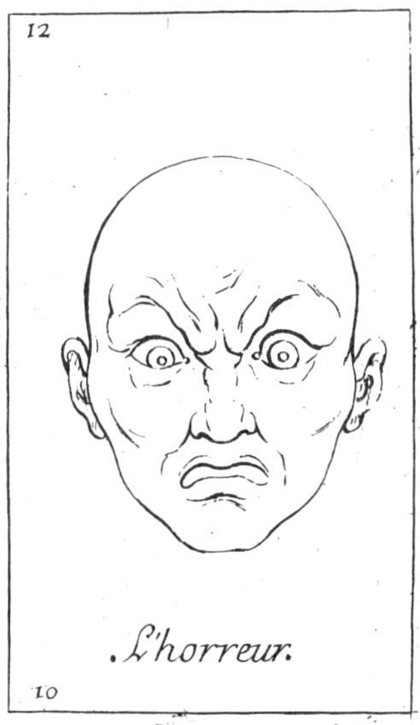

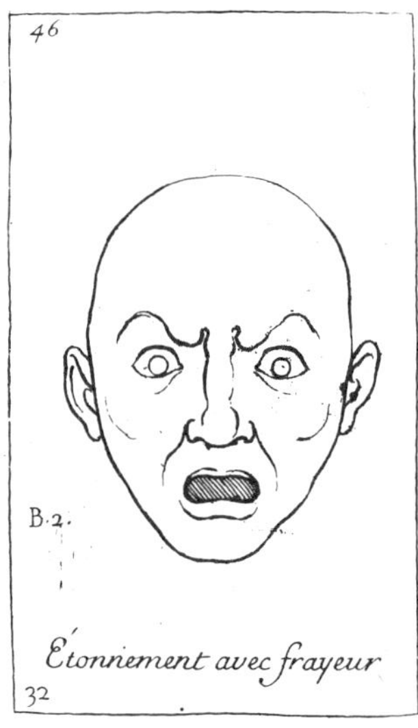

21 Face of Henry IV from Lavater's *Physiognomy*

John Caspar Lavater (1741–1801) was a Swiss clergyman, theologian, and poet whose *Aphorisms on Man* (1788), translated by his and Blake's mutual friend, Henry Fuseli, stimulated some of Blake's most revealing annotations. The *Essays in Physiognomy* appeared in at least fifty-five editions in several countries in the forty years after its first publication in German in 1778. In England by the 1770s there were twelve English versions in five different translations, the most elegant being the Henry Hunter translation (1789–98), which sold for thirty guineas a set.[17] Fuseli sponsored the English edition of 1789 and also designed illustrations for it. He was an enthusiastic supporter of Lavater's studies in physiognomy and a frequent adapter of his models of expression in paintings.[18]

Like LeBrun, Lavater was concerned with the relation between internal feeling and external expression:

> One of the chief ends I have in view in this work is to prove that there is a physionomy; to demonstrate that the physionomy is true; in other words that it is the real and visible expression of internal qualities, which are of themselves invisible.[19]

Blake too perceived an indivisible relationship between mind and body, commenting in *All Religions Are One* "[that] the Poetic Genius is True Man and that the body or outward form of Man is derived from the Poetic Genius." In Lavater, Blake found the system of description of physiognomy described as part of a *language*:

> I do not promise, for it would be the height of folly to make such a promise, to give entire, the immense Alphabet necessary to decypher the original language of Nature, written on the face of Man, and on the whole of his Exterior; but I flatter myself I have been so happy as to trace *a few of the characters* of that divine Alphabet, and that they will be so legible, that a sound eye will readily distinguish them wherever they occur.[20]

To turn page after page of Lavater's minute analyses of eyes, noses, lips, and general facial expressions, including his comments on illustrations after LeBrun and others, is to understand how Blake could adapt for himself a basic code in which lineaments of faces and hands were all "descriptive of character." Blake appears to have borrowed the face of Henry IV of France from a page in Lavater (figure 21, number 16) for one of the beast faces of the *Whore of Babylon* (1809; see Butlin, plate 485). Lavater's description of the face asserted:

> Naturally great, this face is totally degraded, and presents a mere changeling – an image which, realized, would draw tears from the physionomist who is the friend of humanity.[21]

THE LANGUAGE OF THE HANDS

Nature & Art in this together Suit
What is Most grand is always most Minute
Rubens thinks tables Chairs & Stools are grand
But Rafael thinks a Head a foot a hand (Blake's *Notebook*, E 513).

In the seventeenth century, a scholar named John Bulwer undertook a systematic investigation of gestures of the hand. It was called *Chirologia: or the Natural Language of the Hand and Chironomia: or the Art of Manual Rhetoric* and published in 1644. As its modern editor, James Cleary, notes, it was "the first English treatise devoted exclusively to gesticulation and the first to explain the execution of certain gestures by means of chirograms which picture the positions of the hands and fingers."[22] *Chirologia ... Chironomia* is actually two essays, the *Chironomia* an extension of the first essay, concentrating on the importance of gestures of the fingers to the art of rhetoric. The titles are themselves expressive of the intent of the book: *chirologia* is a Latinized word derived from two Greek works meaning "hand" and "law." Bulwer evidently coined the term *chirologia* and Quintilian the word *chironomia*. The work seems to have served as a basis for subsequent treatises, such as Obadiah Walker's *Art of Oratory* (1659), and in spite of the fact that there were only two editions (1644 and 1648), Bulwer's material appears in many works on discourse throughout the eighteenth century, chiefly (though unacknowledged) in Gilbert Austin's *Chironomia* (1806).[23]

Although I can only speculate that Blake may have known Bulwer's *Chirologia*, the traditions of gesture were very much alive on the stage and in acting manuals. Thomas Wilkes, in *A General View of the Stage* (London 1759), had written in his chapter on the art of acting reminiscent of a passage in Bulwer:

All Action wherein the hands are not concerned is weak and limited; Their expressions are as various as language; They speak of themselves, they demand, they promise, call, threaten, implore, detest, fear, question and deny. They express joy, sorrow, doubt, acknowledgement, repentence, moderation; they rouse up, prohibit and prove, admire and abash! All nations, all mankind understand their language. (page 42)

Note the similarity of the following passage in DuFresnoy's *Observations on the Art of Painting* regarding hands. Both Wilkes and DuFresnoy are echoing Bulwer:

Their Motions, which are almost infinite, make innumerable Expressions. Is it not by them, that we desire, that we hope, that we promise, that we call toward us, and that we reject? Besides, they are the Instruments of our threats, of our

22 Blake, *Job*, plate 4

Petitions, of the Horror which we show for things, and of the praises which we give them. By them we fear, we ask Questions, we approve, and we refuse, we show our Joy, and our Sadness, our Doubts, and our Lamentations, our Concernments of Pity, and our Admirations. In short, it may be said, that they are the Language of the Dumb, that they contribute not a little to the speaking of the universal tongue common to all the World, which is that of Painting.[24]

We see here that the language of the hands is being claimed by both painters and actors.

The language of the hands was indeed widely used in instruction manuals for actors and orators. Gilbert Austin's *Chironomia* was even illustrated with gestures employed by Mrs Siddons. Austin invented a method of annotation to indicate how to move when acting or reciting. His chapter XIII, "Of the Positions and Motions of the Hands," used clear illustrations of hand positions important to orators, more than likely copied from Bulwer. I will argue that while Blake was from the beginning using bodily attitudes and hand gestures with an awareness of the tradition (which goes back to Cicero and Quintilian), his *Job* engraving (executed after Austin's publication in 1806) show a special and particular emphasis on hand positions.[25] Indeed, as will be demonstrated, several of Blake's designs seem to be based on illustrations in the earlier *Chirologia*.

Bulwer, and after him, Austin, go to the same ancient sources in describing the use of gesture – Plutarch, Suetonius, Horace, and others; and in examining movement, to Quintilian and Ludovicus Cresollius, the seventeenth-century French Ciceronian rhetorician.[26] Cleary provides a table listing the authors and works that Bulwer cites most frequently – he counts 650 examples and illustrations altogether – and finds that the Bible is cited 214 times.[27]

Among the most "oratorical" of Blake's designs are those of *Job*, designs where narrative is hinted at by the biblical texts provided but where the rich detail of the designs tells us much more than the text alone suggests. Examples from Bulwer's *Chirologia ... Chironomia* can be fruitfully compared with some of the *Job* engravings. The comparison shows Blake frequently exemplifying Bulwer's language of gesture. Consider, for instance, plate 4 of *Job*, where each character, the messenger, Job's wife, and Job, is using his or her hands in an expressive manner (see figure 22). Job's hands may be compared to x in the *Chironomia*'s rhetorical alphabet (see figure 23), which is interpreted thus:

Canon XL
Both hands extended out forward together in an action commodious for them who submit, invoke, doubt, speak to, accuse, or call by name, implore, or attest.

With this action are such as these to be set off to the best of utterance: [You, O hills and groves of Alba; you I say, do I implore and call to witness! And that addubitation of Gra-chus: Wretch that I am, whither shall I betake me? Where

23 Bulwer, from *Chirologia*

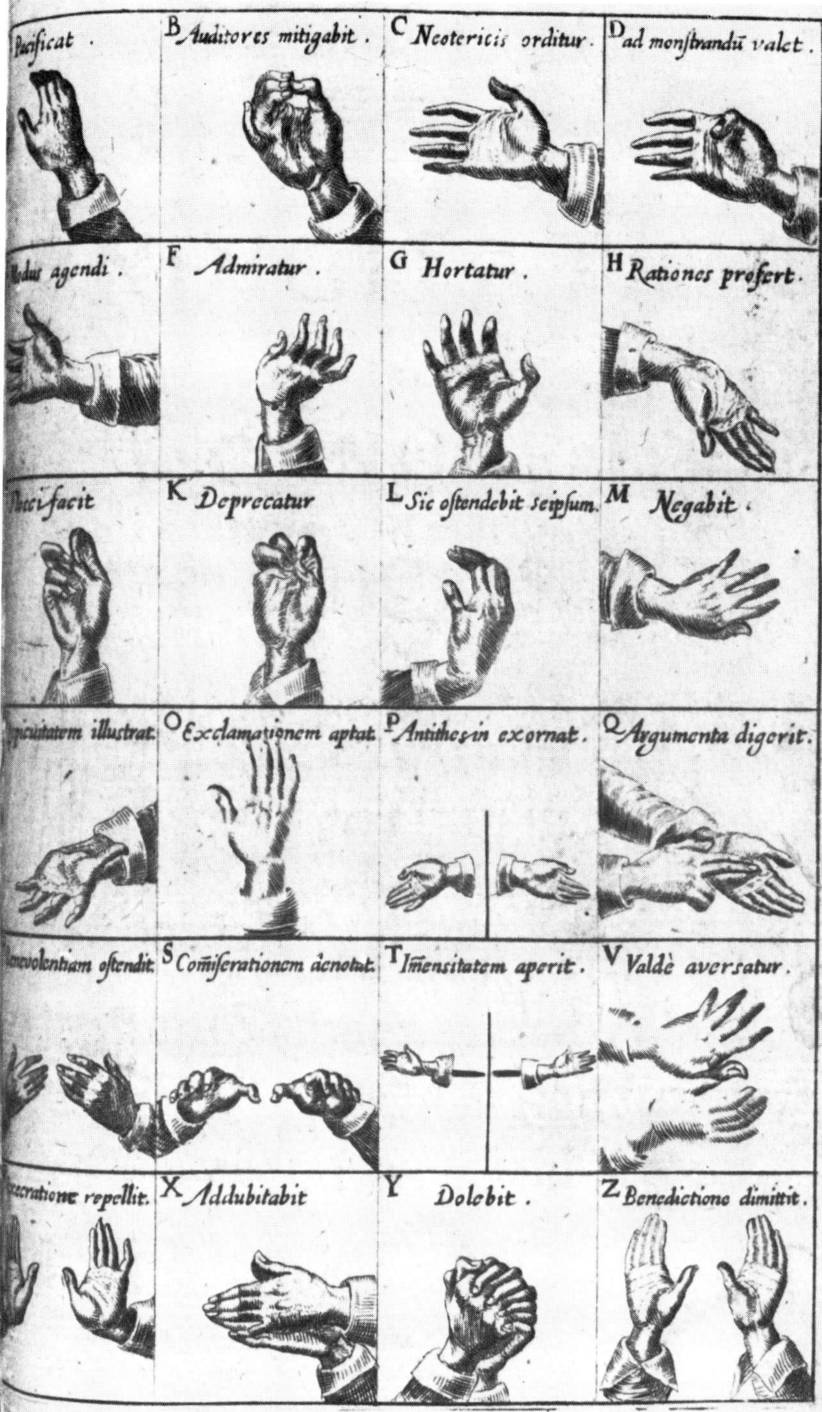

24 Bulwer, from *Chirologia*

shall I turn? To the Capitol? But it flows with the blood of my brother. Or home? etc.][28]

This seems a particularly appropriate response for Job to be making at the horrific announcement of the messenger, although two other gestures from *Chirologia* could also have been adapted here by Blake. These are *Gestus I: Supplico* ("I entreat") and *Gestus II: Oro* ("I pray"). These gestures appear as A and B in the alphabet of natural expressions (see figure 24). The account of *Gestus I: Supplico* begins:

The stretching out of the hands is a natural expression of gesture, wherein we significantly *importunate, entreat, request, sue, solicit, beseech* and ask *mercy or grace* at the hands of others.[29]

The description of *Gestus II: Oro* is also relevant to the situation in plate 4:

To raise the hand conjoined or spread out towards heaven is the habit of *devotion*, in a natural and universal form of *prayer* practised by those who are in *adversity* and in *bitter anguish of mind*, and by those who *give public thanks and praise to the most high*. Thus we *acknowledge our offences, ask mercy, beg relief, pay our vows, imprecate, complain, submit, invoke, and are suppliant*.[30]

Though we are able to interpret Job's gesture without Bulwer, since it

25 LeBrun, *A Method to Learn to Design the Passions: Sadness, Dejection, Sadness and Dejection from the Heart*

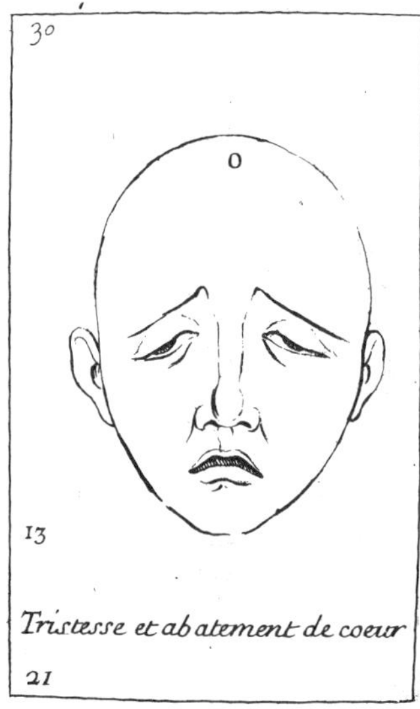

is one which is still in use in churches and on the stage, the gesture of Job's wife in plate 4 is more unusual, and here Blake's meaning is again illuminated by the *Chirologia*. Job's wife's gesture is C in the diagram, *Gestus III: Ploro* ("I weep"; see figure 24). It is described as a natural expression of excessive grief. Her expression here may also be usefully compared to LeBrun's Sadness (figure 25; note especially LeBrun's description of eyelids, nostrils, and mouth: "the Eye-lids fallen and somewhat swelled, the Round of the Eyes livid, the Nostrils drawing downwards, the Mouth somewhat open and the corners down ..." *Method*, page 40).

Bo Lindberg writes that "Job's lifted eyes and clasped hands show the pathos-formula for dismay subdued by piety,"[31] but surely, since Job's hands are distinctly not clasped, while his wife's are (the clasped hands signifying weeping), his open-fingers prayer-gesture is an entreaty suggesting anguish, as Bulwer's description of the gesture suggests, and his dismay is not really subdued.[32]

The gesture of the messenger in *Job* 4 also deserves our attention. The messenger gestures with his left hand as well as his right, which is untraditional for an orator.[33] The right hand points, while the left-hand gesture corresponds to Bulwer's *Gestus XIV: Protego* ("I protect"; figure 24), one meaning of which is described as *warning*:

26 Blake, *Tiriel Carried by Ijim*, drawing no. 7.

To extend out the right hand by the arm foreright is the natural habit wherein we sometimes allure, invite, speak to, cry after, call, or warn to come, bring into, exhort, give warning ...[34]

This is one gesture which Blake apparently used deliberately, with awareness of traditional meaning, in one of his designs in 1789, *Tiriel Carried by Ijim*, drawing 7 of *Tiriel*[35] (see figure 26). Although Bentley believes that Tiriel was cursing his sons and daughters by this gesture, it is more likely in this drawing that he was calling, warning, or admonishing them – because he is using his left hand – "Come forth sons of the curse."[36] In drawing 8 (figure 27), he *is* shown raising his right arm to curse, but the cursing gesture Blake used in later years can be seen in the drawing *Tiriel Denouncing His Sons and Daughters*, consisting of both arms forward.[37] However, in his early days Blake did not pay as much attention to hand details as he did later, and Tiriel's "cursing" hands in drawing 8 are not as expressive as those of Job's mocking friends in *Job* 10, *The Just Upright Man is laughed to scorn* (figure 28).

Since *Job* 10 is one of Blake's most powerful designs and one in which hands are a focal point of both meaning and composition, it is interesting to note there, too, to what extent Blake is working within a tradition.

27 Blake, *Tiriel Supporting the Dying Myratana and Cursing His Sons*, drawing no. 8

28 Blake, *Job*, plate 10, *The Just Upright Man is laughed to scorn*

29 Bulwer, from *Chirologia*

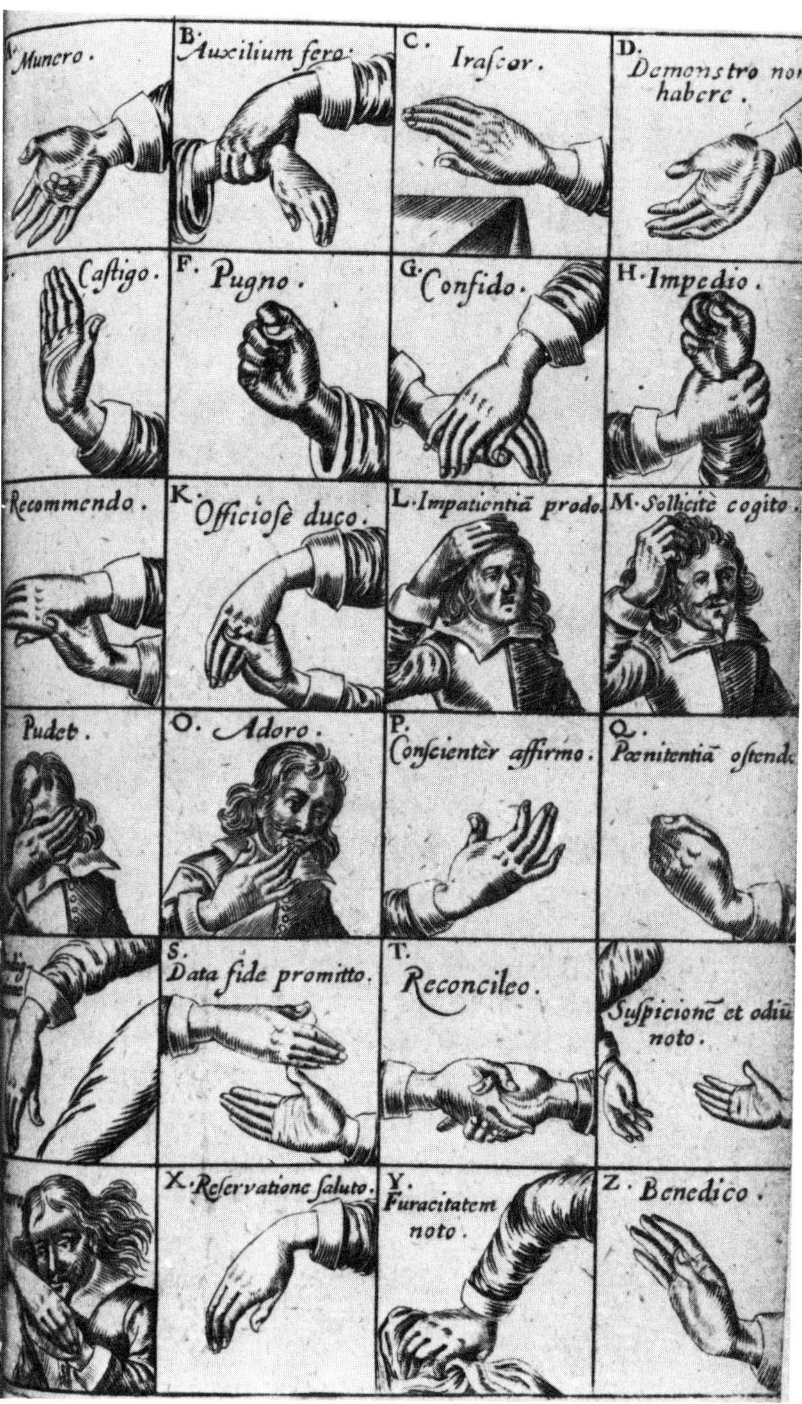

Bo Lindberg notes that in this design some of the hands seem to be copied directly from Giulio Romano's *The Adoration of Shepherds*, engraved by Marcantonio's pupil, Agostino Venetiano, in 1521.[38] Since the meaning of the gesture in that picture is ostensibly the very opposite of what it means in *Job* 10, Lindberg also needs to remark that Romano's painting was peculiar in adopting pointing fingers as an expression of adoration. But if we look closely at Romano's picture, we see that the "adoring" shepherd is *not* pointing with his index or saluting finger but with his middle finger. In *Chirologia* Bulwer notes that the ancient posture of adoration had the "saluting finger laid over-thwart the thumb." And the shepherd who *is* pointing is obviously demonstrating to another, not adoring. Romano also apparently knew the ancient traditions. I think we can assume that if Blake did adopt from Romano the general formula of gesticulating figures in a row, he deliberately made his hand gestures conform to the meaning of scorn he wished to communicate and adapted the gesture *Respuo* ("I reject"; see figure 24) described in *Chirologia*:

> Gestus XX: Respuo
> The flirting out of the back part of the hand or put-by of the turning palm is their natural expression who would refuse, deny, prohibit, repudiate, impute, or to lay to one's charge, reject or ... would twit and hit one in the teeth with a thing, and signify disdain.[39]

We can see that Blake's treatment of hands in *Job* 10 is much more vivacious than that of the model from *Chirologia*, and there are differences between the right and left hands of Job's friends that must be observed. I would suggest that the prominent backs of the hands take their meaning from *Respuo* (Eliphaz is still prominently displaying the back of his hand to indicate that he does not like what Elihu says in *Job* 12, for example)[40] but that the rather gracefully pointing right hands of Job's friends constitute a gesture derived from Michelangelo's hand of God on the Sistine ceiling which I have previously called "creative fingers." They can as well suggest the casting of a spell or the creation of an error.[41]

Job's wife also displays the backs of her hands in a rather unusual gesture which may be Blake's adaptation of Bulwer's canon XXXIV, *Valde Aversatur* ("Exceedingly turned away"; see figure 23), which accompanies words of "detestation, despite, and exprobation."[42] If this is so, it is a touch of characterization: beyond her weeping, she is defending Job against his scorning friends.

Job's open-handed gesture in this design can suggest his liberality and free heart: the gesture is named *Munero* ("I reward"; see A, figure 29). This gesture corresponds to the words at the top of the design, "But he knoweth the way that I take / when he hath tried me I shall come forth like gold," and "though he slay me yet will I trust in him."

A glance at the evolution of *Job* 10 reveals Blake's interest in hand gestures becoming more specific over the years. The earliest version Blake composed of this scene was a pen-and-wash drawing of 1785 (figure 30) in which all the hand gestures of the characters are different from the later versions. The sepia painting of 1793 shows some changes: here Job is depicted with open hands, his wife with clasped hands, and Eliphaz pointing under his beard with one hand. These hand gestures do not change for the engraved version of 1793[43] (see figure 31). However, the final versions of this design as *Job* 10 – Butts's watercolour, Linnell's watercolour, and the engraving – change radically the gestures of Job's friends and his wife, while keeping the 1793 position of Job himself. All this suggests that by 1806, when the Butts set was painted, Blake had decided on the meaning of these hand positions and was paying careful attention to the meaning of the hands.[44] It was in 1810 also that he wrote those words which are now so familiar to devotees of Blake's art but which seem particularly relevant to this study of minute discriminations:

> I intreat then that the Spectator will attend to the Hands & Feet to the Lineaments of the Countenances they are all descriptive of character & not a line is drawn without intention & that most discriminate and particular (E 560).

30 Blake, *Job, his wife and his friends*, 1785

LANGUAGES OF THE BODY

Dramatic Gesture

Not only hands and faces but also bodily gestures or attitudes were categorized in the eighteenth century, and we will now look at some of the other material on the subject of gesture that Blake is likely to have known and made use of. Of course, the raising of a hand and arm itself constitutes a bodily gesture, and these have been discussed in the previous pages: now we move to demonstrate how techniques of acting, dramatic gesture, and dance influenced Blake's designs.

We can see Blake's interest in "body language" (to adapt the modern term slightly out of context) in two pages of sketches, now at Harvard University (see figures 32 and 33), called *Various Personifications, A Death Bed and Other Drawings*.[45] Here Blake appears to be trying out various attitudes which will symbolize states of mind. They may be sketches for figures he was to use in the designs for Young's *Night Thoughts*, where so

31 Blake, *Job: What is Man That thou shouldst Try him Every Moment?* 1793

many of the figures are representative of thoughts or moods. The attempt to express feelings through a position of the body allies Blake's activity with similar attempts of a play director or a ballet master.

A useful relationship to keep in mind when observing Blake's attitudes for the body is the link between the acting and painting styles of his time. As Alastair Smart has noted, the declamatory gestures of a Garrick or a Siddons would embarrass us today, just as the same gestures in painting would leave us unimpressed, "for it is easy to mistake the same language of gesture, as it was used by the painters, for empty rhetoric and bombast."[46] But it was not empty rhetoric, for the conventions of theatrical gesture were closely related to the language of gesture used by painters, who in turn were constantly turning to antique sculpture for inspiration. Thus we see the many portraits of the English aristocracy in the attitudes of the Apollo Belvedere or ancient nymphs. Emma Hamilton's "attitudes" – her poses in imitation of Greek sculpture and vase paintings – were one of the famous amusements of the Hamilton circle in Italy in the 1780s and later in London.[47] Brian Reade, in his compendium of ballet designs, writes of Emma:

> The attitudes, or mimes were based upon the postures of figures in Antique Gems and sculptures. In his *Italienishe Reise*, Goethe records spending two happy

32 Blake, *Various Personifications, A Death Bed and Other Drawings* (recto)

evenings at Naples in 1787, watching Emma Hamilton bring to life – so he felt – the female figures in Greek and Roman works of art. She was, in fact, a Neoclassic mime, or poseuse, and though her performances were entirely domestic, they had a little of the same value as stimuli to artists as the eurhythmics of Isadora Duncan a century later.[48]

This influence may be seen to extend to students of drawing, who in 1797 could purchase a book by the artist Friedrich Rehberg called *Lady Hamilton's Attitudes*, published by a firm in London advertised as a place "Where Prints and Drawings are lent to Copy By the Year, Quarter, Month, etc."[49] (see figure 34). In 1801 the same firm published *A Second Part to Lady Hamilton's Attitudes*, containing "Outlines of Figures and Drapery collected with great care from Ancient Statues, Monuments, Bas Relievos, Forming an useful and necessary Study for Amateurs in Drawing: From the most correct and chaste Models of Grecian and Roman Sculpture, Nero, Berenice, Orestes, Pylades, Hermione, etc."

Blake's friend and patron George Cumberland kept an album of his own copies of antique and Renaissance sculpture, some carefully coloured in the black and red of vase painters, categorized by himself as to kinds of gesture or motion, as, for instance, "dancing motion," "floating motion," "violent action," "enthusiastic action."[50] The English artists who

33 Blake, *Various Personifications, A Death Bed and Other Drawings* (verso)

visited Rome in the 1770s – a group including Fuseli, Flaxman, Barry, and Mortimer – evolved a discernible style of their own from the inspiration of gestures in the monuments and paintings of the Villa Albani and the Villa Medici. Henry Fuseli, most notably a painter of dramatic and exaggerated gesture, had probably the most profound influence on this aspect of Blake's art. Peter Tomory, speaking of gesture in Fuseli's work, remarks:

> He often employs, for instance, the clenched hand, the knuckles whitened with the intensity of the emotion, whether it is in his *Self-Portrait* or in *The Death of a Cardinal Beaufort*. Inevitably he pays close attention to the positions of fingers in a hand gesture, the best example being of *Balaam* from Lavater's Essays (French ed. c. 1778) ... the *Monstrari digito* and its less articulated companions appear in extraordinary variety through *King Lear* and others to *Gray's Bard* ...[51]

The pointing finger – *monstrari digito* – is as we have seen of great importance in Blake's vocabulary of gesture too, though Fuseli seems to express all artists' debt to the antique on this subject in his drawing *The Artist in despair over the magnitude of Antique Fragments* (circa 1770–80;

34 Lady Hamilton in two of her "attitudes," from *Lady Hamilton's Attitudes* by F. Rehberg, 1797

illustrated in Tomory, page 54), which shows a huge pointing finger and a huge foot quite overwhelming the poor artist.

The close connection between the stage gestures of actors, painting, and oratory was a favourite topic of those involved in both the production of drama and the instruction of painting. No doubt the link between painting and the stage was through oratory and the belief that gesture was a universal language. Betterton, in a long passage on the meaning of gestures, stated:

> Gesture has therefore this Advantage above mere Speaking, that by this we are understood by those of our own Language, but by Action and Gesture (I mean just and regular Action) we make our Thoughts and Passions intelligible to all Nations and Tongues. It is ... the common Speech of Mankind ...[52]

Thomas Wilkes in *A General View of the Stage* recommended the aspiring actor to study historical paintings for character, dress and manner, as had Thomas Betterton before him.[53] Actors followed their advice. Hogarth's painting of *Garrick as Richard III* in the tent scene, his arm outstretched in horror, his fingers extended, shows Garrick following the rules for that passion as described by Wilkes.[54]

Behind both Betterton and Wilkes was the work of Obadiah Walker, whose *The Art of Oratory* (London 1659) had described, in the manner of *Chirologia*, a kind of stage direction for the speaker:

> Arms should be drawn back close to the sides, when requesting: putting out the *fore-finger*, when demonstrating, and as it were showing a thing (therefore is that finger called the Index). So the hand is put forward with the thumb bended in for demonstrating. The *first* finger turned down for urgency and pressing as it were: *put up* for threatening: the middle finger put out for reproaching: the *left thumb* touched by the Index of the right hand for reasoning, and disputing: the touching of *a finger* with the *other hand*, for distinguishing and for numbering. The hand brought *toward one*, in saying anything of himself; *toward the head*, when speaking of the understanding; to the breast when of the soul, will or affections. *Folding* the arms in sadness etc., and lastly: one, and that no small, service of the *Hand* is, that it *keeps time*, in our speech, with our periods ...[55]

Not surprisingly, oratorical tradition had become partly visual. Both Fuseli and Blake paint scenes and characters from Shakespeare, Fuseli of course being a significant contributor to publisher John Boydell's eleven-volume National Edition of Shakespeare (1791–1805), and there is surely a relation between the exaggerated gesture and expression of Fuseli's designs and the exaggerated, not to say violent, acting of Kemble and Mrs Siddons.[56] And behind the acting traditions are the handbooks of Betterton, Wilkes, and Aaron Hill, all instructing in the proper motions of the hands and arms and bodies, and expressions of the face. Among the most theatrical of Blake's designs in this respect are his illustrations to the poems of Thomas Gray.[57] These designs, executed between 1797 and 1798, demonstrate a Fuseli-like expansiveness of gesture, as do many of the designs for Young's *Night Thoughts*.[58]

Pantomime

In this sketch of the kinds of visual languages that made up the context within which Blake's designs emerge, pantomime plays a not insignificant role. In England there was a traditional love of pantomime. Blake was bound to have seen a pantomime if he went to dramatic performances. Ordinary plays were often followed by the antics and dances of Punch, Scaramouche, and Harlequin, which eventually became more popular than the dramas themselves.[59] Pantomime provides a link between the oral tradition and the visual expression of the Passions. For example, during the eighteenth century the English Harlequin had a repertoire of five standard poses, one of which would conclude each phase of mime; poses represented Admiration, Defiance, Determination, Flirtation, and Thought.[60]

The first person to write about pantomimes in England was the dancing master John Weaver, who published *The History of the Mimes and Pantomimes* in 1728.[61] This work is of interest to us for what it has to say about gesture and the Passions. I will demonstrate what appears to me to be a strong connection between Weaver's description of pantomimic gestures and Blake's depiction, in biblical designs executed circa 1800–5, of similar passions.

Weaver wished to improve the level of performance in England:

> The Town having for some Years past run into *Dramatick* Entertainments, consisting of *Dancing*, *Gesture*, and *Action*, intermix'd with *Trick* and *Show*; and to which they have given the Name of *Pantomimes*: I am apt to persuade myself, that an Historical Account of the ancient *Mimes* and *Pantomimes* of the *Greeks* and *Romans*, will ... render the Spectator better capable of Judging these modern performances. (page 2)

Weaver believed modern performance had degenerated, especially in Italy. He maintained that the English, though capable of improvement, were doing better because "*ours* are Representations of entire Stories, carried on by various *Motions*, *Action* and *dumb Show*" (page 4). (Weaver himself is reputed to have introduced the silent Harlequin to the English stage, though actor-manager John Rich became famous in the role.) Weaver's description of the pantomimers of the ancient world contains the eighteenth-century man's admiration for the dramatic imitation of the passions. In this passage the words *mimes* and *pantomimes* refer to dancers themselves:

> The Mimes and Pantomimes, tho' Dancers, had their Names from *Acting*, that is, from *Imitation*; *copying* all the *Force* of the *Passions* meerly by the *Motions* of the

Body to that degree, as to draw Tears from the *Audience* at their Representations. 'Tis true, that with the *Dancing*, the *Musick* sung a Sort of *Opera* or *Songs* on the same *Subject*, which the *Dancer* performed; yet what was chiefly *minded*, and carried away with the *Esteem* and *Applause* of the Audience was the *Action* of the *Pantomimes*, when they performed *without* the Help of *Musick*, *Vocal* or *Instrumental*.

These *Pantomimes* were *Imitators of all Persons and of Things*, as the Name imports; and performed by *Gesture*, and the *Action* of Hands, Legs, and Feet, without making use of *Tongue* in uttering their Thoughts; and in this Performance the Hands and Fingers were much made use of, and expressed perhaps a *large share* of the Performance. *Aristotle* says, that they imitated by *Number* alone without Harmony: for they imitated the Manner, Passions and Actions by the *numerous* Variety of Gesticulation ... (pages 7–8)

Weaver published the "scripts" of his own productions, and they contain rare accounts of how his dancers moved. For *The Loves of Mars and Venus* (performed at the Theatre Drury Lane in 1717) he wrote a long description of each emotion:

This last Dance being altogether of the Pantomimic kind; it is necessary that the Spectator should know some of the most particular Gestures made use of therein; and what Passions or Affections, they discover; represent; or express.

Admiration
Admiration is discover'd by the raising up of the right Hand, the Palm turn'd upwards, the Fingers clos'd; and in one Motion the Wrist turn'd round and Fingers spread; the Body reclining, and Eyes fix'd on the Object; but when it rises to

Astonishment
Both Hands are thrown up towards the Skies; the Eyes also lifted up, and the Body cast backwards.

Jealousy
Jealousy will appear by the Arms suspended, or a particular pointing the middle Finger to the Eye, by an irresolute Movement throughout the Scene, and a Thoughtfulness of Countenance.

Upbraiding
The Arms thrown forwards; the Palm of the Hands turn'd outward; the Fingers open, and the Elbows turn'd inward to the Breast; shew Upbraiding, and Despite.

Anger
The left Hand struck suddenly with the right, and sometimes against the Breast; denotes Anger.

Threats
Threatning, is express'd by raising the Hand, and shaking the bended Fist;

knitting the Brow; biting the Nails; and catching back the Breath.

Power
The Arm, with impetuous Agitation, directed forwards to the Person, with an awful Look, implies Authority.

Impatience
Impatience is seen by the smiting of the Thigh, or Breast with the Hand.

Indignation
When it rises to Anguish, and Indignation, it is express'd by applying the Hand passionately to the Forehead; or by stepping back the right Foot, leaning the Body quite backward, the Arms extended, Palms clos'd, and Hands thrown quite back; the Head cast back, and Eyes fix'd upwards.

These are some of the Actions made use of by Vulcan; those by Venus are as follows.

Coquetry
Coquetry will be seen in affected Airs, given her self throughout the whole Dance.

Neglect
Neglect will appear in the scornful turning the Neck; the flirting outward the back of the right Hand, with a Turn of the Wrist.

Contempt
Contempt is express'd by scornful Smiles; forbidding Looks; tossing of the Head; filliping of the Fingers; and avoiding the Object.

Distaste
The left Hand thrust forth with the Palm turn'd backward; the left Shoulder rais'd, and the Head bearing towards the Right, denotes an Abhorrence, and Distaste.

Detestation
When both the turn'd-out Palms are so bent to the left Side, and the Head still more projected from the Object; it becomes a more passionate Form of Detestation, as being a redoubled Action.

Triumph
To Shake the Hand open, rais'd above our Head, is an exulting Expression of Triumph.

Entreaty
The stretching out the Hand downward toward the knees is an Action of Entreaty, and Suing for mercy.[62]

These instructions are similar to those we have seen in Bulwer's *Chirologia* and attest to the wide application of these traditions of movement and gesture. There are many figures in Blake's work which echo a Weaver-like pantomime. For example, both of Weaver's descriptions for

Admiration and Astonishment fit the two women on either side of Christ in Blake's watercolour *The Raising of Lazarus* (circa 1805; Butlin, plate 561). Similarly posed is Mary in the *Paradise Regained* design *Christ Returns to His Mother* (figure 35). An even more vivid example of Astonishment is found in *The Ghost of Samuel Appearing to Saul* (circa 1800; Butlin, plate 539), where Saul is depicted with the raised hands, lifted eyes, and body cast backwards.

35 Blake, *Paradise Regained: Christ Returns to His Mother*

Weaver's Entreaty can be seen in Blake's *David Pardoning Absalom* (circa 1800–3; Butlin, plate 540), where Absalom's hands are stretched out and downwards towards the knees. (David's palms, incidentally, are in the open-handed position called *Munero* ["I reward"] in the *Chirologia*.) And one of Weaver's descriptions of Indignation, "when it rises to Anguish," is the gesture of hands passionately applied to the forehead made by Lamech in *Lamech and His Two Wives* (Butlin, plate 391) and by Cain in *The Body of Abel Found by Adam and Eve* (circa 1805–9; Butlin, plate 596). This gesture then reminds us of the link between Lamech and Cain, Lamech being Cain's great-great-great-grandson (Gen. 4: 23–4). The second part of Weaver's descriptions of Indignation ("leaning the Body quite backward, the Arms extended ... hands thrown quite back ...") may be seen in Blake's *Moses Indignant at the Golden Calf* (Butlin, plate 487).

It is not necessary for Blake to have read Weaver to be using these gestures; but it is apparent that the code of meanings for gestures in both dance and painting was part of the general lore understood by artists in these fields.

The languages of gesture we have briefly surveyed here have covered the fields of painting, oratory, acting, and mime.[63] Blake's knowledge of some of this material is speculative, of some probable, but it is undeniable that the naming and categorizing of gesture and attitude in the arts was an eighteenth-century obsession, and we will see again and again that Blake made use of these traditions in his designs.

APPENDIX

The Domestic Images: The Decorative Arts

In the autumn of 1784, William Blake and James Parker, who had both apprenticed as engravers with James Basire, went into business together at 27 Broad Street in London. Blake was young – twenty-six years old – and two years married to Catherine Boucher. His father had died in July, and the legacy enabled Blake to enter the print-selling and -publishing business, with shop and house on the same premises, shared, it appears, with the Parkers. He must have been full of hope and energy. It was a time that he was to use as a landmark when, twenty years later, after long mental and economic struggle, he found his energies reawakened:

> Suddenly, on the day after visiting the Truchsessian Gallery of Pictures, I was again enlightened with the light I enjoyed in my youth and which has for exactly twenty years been closed from me ... (Letter to Hayley, 23 October 1804; E 756)

Some critics feel that the twenty years beginning in 1784 were bleak because Blake was relatively unsuccessful in the world of commerce ("I was a slave bound in a mill among beasts and devils"), and in retrospect he felt that his energies had been deflected from the spiritual. No doubt his disillusion sprang from many sources, but the world of commerce, as far as the printing trades went, was at an exciting juncture in 1784, and Blake was surely caught up in it.

Expansion was evident in all the book trades: the number of master printers in London almost doubled in the twenty years from 1784 to 1804; there were fifty-three print-sellers in London by 1802, where there had been only fourteen in 1785. In this same period the number of engravers increased from 48 to 203 and booksellers from 151 to 308.[1] Some of this expansion may be attributed to the relatively peaceful first decade of the young William Pitt's ministry (1783–93), which stimulated commerce. In 1800 Blake wrote to George Cumberland, recalling the business enterprise when print shops were rare:

> There are now I believe as many Booksellers as there are Butchers & as many Printshops as of any other trade We remember when a Print shop was a rare bird in London & I myself remember when I thought my pursuits of Art a kind of Criminal Dissipation & neglect of the main chance which I hid my face for not being able to abandon as a Passion which is forbidden by Law & Religion, but now it appears to be Law & Gospel too ... (2 July 1800; E 706)

Parker and Blake are known to have published only two prints on their own, *Zephyrus and Flora* and *Callisto*, engraved by Blake after his friend, the painter Thomas Stothard. Erdman writes of good reasons for this venture: "Fortunes were being made on single issues – for print-seller if not for artist or engraver. An engraving of Fuseli's *Night Mare* in 1783 brought the publisher £500."[2] Unfortunately, Parker and Blake did not make their fortunes on their prints: their "decently erotic and discreetly naked Floras and Venuses," as Erdman neatly calls them, obviously did not have the shock value of Fuseli's disturbing picture.

Involvement in the book trade in London in the eighteenth century, as Blake experienced as an engraver, meant involvement not only with the stationers, bookbinders, paper-stainers (who made wallpapers), copper-plate merchants, and rag merchants but also with designers of pottery and printed textiles. This thriving activity of artists and artisans was as much a part of Blake's world as the more academic realm of the Royal Academy and the collector. Indeed, the language of forge and loom, mills and wheels so frequent in Blake's poetry is as well grounded in daily life as it is in symbolism.

The English Industrial Revolution affected the decorative arts and thereby the personal surroundings of men and women in a very direct way: the invention of a method to print designs on textiles and china-ware with engraved copper plates made a kind of decoration available to everyone which had formerly been available only to the rich. A floral design appearing on a teapot would be echoed in chintz drapery materials and perhaps on wallpapers as well. A statue might inspire a ceramic figurine like the flowered-robed *Cleopatra*[3] (see Introduction, figure 8). Traditional needlework designs would be adapted to plate-printed textiles (figure 36), or maps would be printed on satin. Engravings of floral arrangements inspired designs for bedspreads. This merging of the visual and applied arts had a deep influence on the development of Blake's work as a "composite art." The repetition of motifs from one medium to another would surely have impressed on him the universality of a language of art that was readily available to all.

As a printer, Blake would have been aware of the growing textile-printing industry centred in the districts around London in the mid-1700s.[4] We know that he knew at least one friend directly involved: a Mr

36 Bedspread: *June*, from *The Twelve Months of Flowers*, 1730

Trotter, a draughtsman to the calico-printers. Alexander Gilchrist, Blake's biographer, says it was he who introduced Blake to Stothard.[5]

The use of engraved copper plates transformed European textile-printing, in which cloth had traditionally been block-printed with col-

37 Blake, *The Book of Thel*, title-page

ours that were not washable. Until 1752, no dyes had been developed suitable to print washable engravings on linen or cotton. It is no wonder, then, that cottons from India, which were printed with washable dyes, became so popular.[6] Once the English textile-printing industry developed the engraved techniques, many designs were based on Indian chintzes. The oriental flavour of the animals and flowers in some of Blake's designs may owe something to his familiarity with these textiles. (See the flower and leaf forms on *Thel's* title-page, or numerous *Paradise Lost* designs, compared to a quilt from India's Coromandel coast [figures 37, 38, and 39].)

38 English bed-curtain, mid-seventeenth century

39 Quilt from India, Coromandel Coast

Mythological scenes were popular with the English designers of plate-printed cottons, and some of these bear strong resemblances to Blake's designs. The *Bromley Hall Pattern Book* (circa 1790)[7] contains a design called *Tyger* showing children riding tigers (figure 40). Comparing this with Blake's *America*, plate 11 (figure 41), we can see familiar figures in the two children riding the snake, and even a similarity in the faces of snake and tiger. The textile is contemporary with *The Book of Thel*, which uses the same *America* design (plate 6) running in a different direction. One wonders if Blake's friend Trotter might be a connecting link here. Certainly the image of children riding or lying down with animals is central to Blake's depiction of Innocence, and other details of this textile design seem quite Blakean. In the upper right corner, for example, a piper sits under a tree while a nursemaid and two children dance.

Another design from *Bromley Hall* is called *Mars* and shows the god clad as a Roman soldier, borne in a chariot by three lions with human faces (figure 42). This design recalls *Jerusalem* 41. I have also come across another cotton which seems very Blakean in theme (figure 43). Its motifs include a traveller with a staff fending off a beast. There is a wonderful mix of jungle foliage, and an English cottage where children are feeding

40 *Bromley Hall Pattern Book: Tyger*

a snake a bowl of milk. Fashionable eighteenth-century ladies appear to watch a fight between a leopard and a stag. A dromedary is prominent in the design, as is a tiger. A man rides an ostrich pursued by hounds, and a wolf (?) tries to shake a leopard (?) from its back. (The techniques of the engraver are obvious in this design, from the bold strokes on the tree

41 Blake, *America*, plate 11

42 *Bromley Hall Pattern Book: Mars*

43 Plate-printed cotton

44 Plate-printed cotton, *The Judgment of Paris*, 1795

45 Blake, *The Judgment of Paris*

trunks and leaves to the finer modelling of the human figures.) The mixture of violence and serenity in the design and the simultaneous action of the repeated activities express a mood not unlike that of the *Songs of Innocence and of Experience*, where the states of Innocence and Experience are often simultaneously present in one design. Yet another of Blake's designs, *The Judgment of Paris*, executed in 1817, bears a strong resemblance to a plate-printed cotton of about 1795 (figures 44 and 45). Barbara J. Morris, who wrote extensively about the English textile designs when they were first discovered, could not find a source for this design but thought it reminiscent of Stothard.[8] Whatever the sources of these allegorical motifs, Blake must have regarded the use of them in a decorative material as a part of the language of art.

There is no known record of Blake's involvement in commercial textile design, although there is one existing example of an engraved tradesman's card which he designed for Moore and Co, a firm which manufactured carpets and hosiery.[9] Since Blake's brother James was a hosier and his father had been one, it is not surprising to see that Blake's design shows a real familiarity with the machinery involved. It seems possible that he would have been more familiar with commercial ventures of this nature than is usually supposed. In the Metropolitan Museum's collection of tradesmen's cards is an eighteenth-century printer's card whose emblem of an eagle closely resembles Blake's eagle in *Milton* (figures 46 and 47).

Engravers also worked for ceramic manufacturers. Transfer printing

46 Trade card, "S. Burton, Stationer"

on ceramic or enamel was a method by which patterns were transferred from an engraved copper plate to the ware by means of a tissue paper printed with special ceramic colours.[10] It is, of course, the name of Josiah Wedgwood which is immediately associated with the design of ceramics in the eighteenth century. Wedgwood Jasperware both reflected and promoted the popular classical revival. Blake's friend John Flaxman designed wax models and tableware in the Wedgwood potteries for Thomas Bentley from 1775 to 1787, his chief source of income in his early career. Flaxman put Blake in touch with Josiah Wedgwood some years

47 Blake, *Milton*, plate 38

later, when Blake executed both drawings and engravings for a catalogue of domestic pottery: 185 figures were engraved on 18 plates.[11] Blake was paid £30 for engraving on 11 November 1816.[12]

An interesting Blakean motif can be found on the handle of a Wedgwood black basalt sugar-bowl cover (figure 48). This hooded figure looks very like Blake's plate 16 from *The Gates of Paradise*, or like Henry Fuseli's *Silence*. And to argue further Blake's familiarity with the applied arts of his time, I would suggest that the enamel-painted designs of birds and flowers which are so familiar a part of fine English porcelains found

48 Wedgwood sugar bowl, about 1800

their way into Blake's depiction of birds of paradise in plates such as *America* 6 or *Job* 2.

Since Blake wrote a good deal about his own capacities for drawing and the quality of his "execution," and since we also know that he could draw in any way he chose – realistically or symbolically – his choice of floral motifs and the sources he chose to emulate are of some importance to an understanding of his purpose. It is possible that he chose the iconographically familiar forms of popular textile and ceramic designs because in this way he might reaffirm a language of art which he firmly believed was all around him ("no one can ever Design till he has learned the Language of Art by making many Finished Copies both of Nature and Art and of what ever comes in his way from Earliest Childhood" – *Annotations to Reynolds*, E 645). The universality of such forms, which transcend linguistic differences, implies a unity in the human imagination which makes all art and all religions one.

PART II

BLAKE'S VISIONARY FORMS

Four Figures

In this section I explore the primary figures in Blake's vocabulary of forms, the recurring attitudes and gestures which bear the nucleus of meaning in so many of his designs. Symbolic meanings tend to cluster around these figures as we become aware of how consistently they are used.

Four clusters of visual images recur most often in Blake's designs, and these I have observed to signify consistent qualities: figures with outstretched arms stand for creativity or, in their fallen state, power perverted to tyranny; huddled and head-clutching figures are symbols of despair; upward-leaping figures signify psychic energy; and dancing figures appear to be symbols of energy of the body, mortal impulses.

In *Anatomy of Criticism*, Northrop Frye defines an *archetype* as "a symbol, usually an image, which recurs often enough in literature to be recognizable as an element of one's literary experience as a whole."[1] The forms I consider here may be called archetypes in an analogous sense, recurring often enough in Blake's work to be recognizable as an element of one's experience of his art. Like his poetic archetypes, Blake's visual images are indicative primarily of *states* of man, which is one reason the human figure in various attitudes is so central to his designs.

HREE

Humanity Divine

THE GESTURE OF OUTSTRETCHED ARMS

Of the various visual images in Blake's designs, this gesture is probably the most frequently observed. Figures with arms in this position (the Latin-cross position – arms extended horizontally, at right angles to the body) can be seen primarily in four poses: standing; seated or kneeling with one knee raised; hovering, with only head and arms visible; and prostrate. Representative examples of these attitudes are, for the standing figure, *Albion Rose* (figure 49); for the raised-knee figure, plate 8 of *America* (figure 50); for the hovering figure, *The Lazar House* (figure 51); for the prostrate figure, Adam in *Elohim Creating Adam* (figure 17). These four forms are discussed in some detail in this section.

There are also other forms which incorporate this gesture: prone or supine figures, flat on the ground, viewed head-on (*A Poison Tree*); and striding figures (*Urizen* 3, *Jerusalem* 26). These, together with further variations – figures with arms outstretched forwards (Elohim in *Elohim Creating Adam*) and figures with arms outstretched at an oblique angle (*Jerusalem* 99) – are considered briefly later. Even from this short list the consistent presence of the gesture in Blake's art is indicated, and as the discussion proceeds I hope to demonstrate that it is an important visual symbol, both eloquent in itself and useful in the interpretation of a poetic text in which the design occurs.

The traditional image suggested by outstretched arms is of course the Cross, a symbol of divinity rich with associations of self-sacrifice or death, and regeneration. The cruciform gesture also carries in Western art traditional connotations of creativity – for example, Michelangelo's *God Creating Adam* or Raphael's God in designs for the Vatican Loggie. Thus the gesture can be seen to be complementary to the main themes of Blake's poetry and thought: man's essential divinity and capacity for regeneration or, from the aspect of fallen vision, man's own error of turning that divine creativity into mental tyranny or spiritual death. Blake appears consistently to associate the gesture with these themes. The four attitudes which repeatedly carry these connotations each have a regenerative and a demonic aspect and can also subtly be distinguished one from another as indicators of mental states. Yet it is always with some aspect of divinity that outstretched arms are associated.

The crucified Christ is a frequent image in Blake's art, his outstretched arms a metaphor for his self-sacrifice. In this Blake follows the iconographic tradition of Western art. His Crucifixion illustrations include *Jerusalem* 76, *The Prophecy of the Crucifixion* (*Paradise Lost*, 1808), and the watercolour design *The Crucifixion: Christ Taking Leave of His Mother*.

49 Blake, *Albion Rose*, line engraving

50 Blake, *America*, plate 8

51 Blake, *The Lazar House*

52 Blake, *Jerusalem*, plate 76

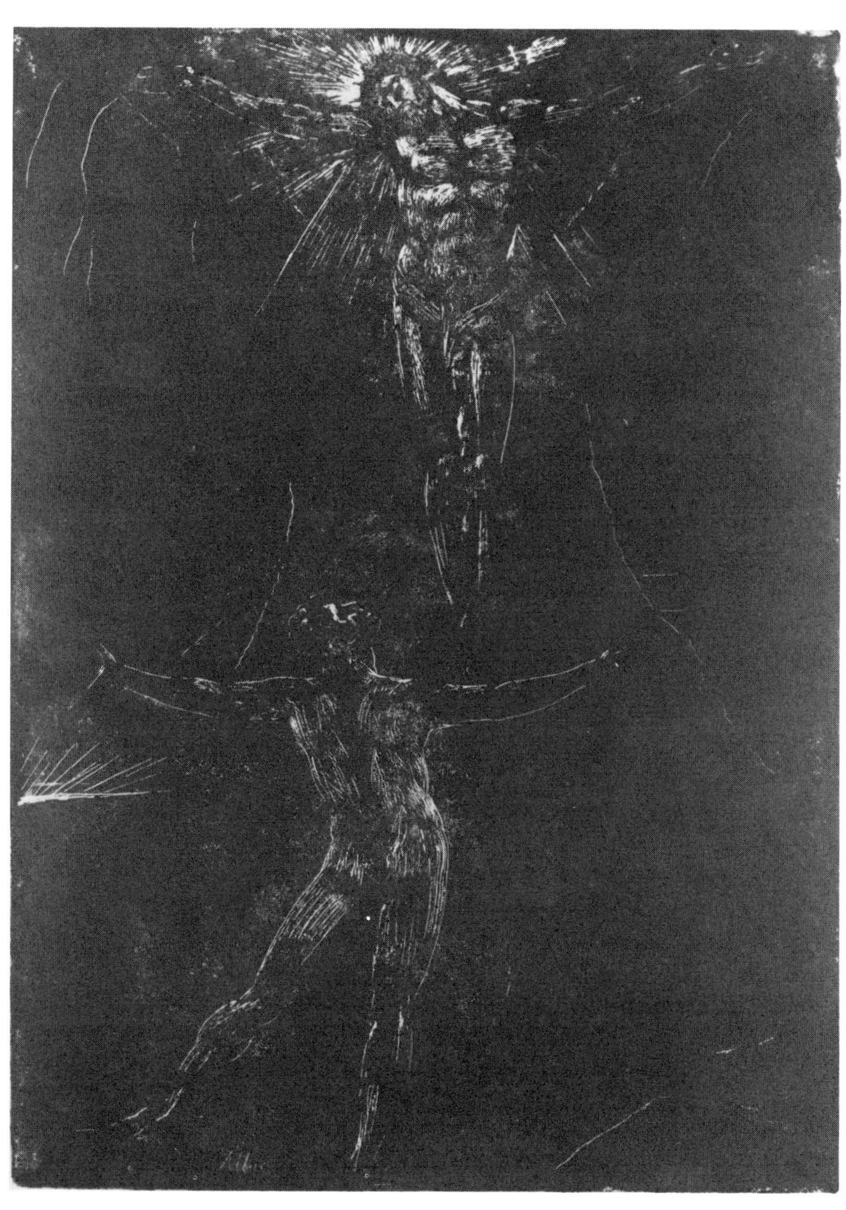

In these designs the sacrificial aspect of the symbol is underlined both by the sadness and passivity of Jesus and by the extended arms nailed to the bar of the Cross. In *Jerusalem* 76 the arms of Albion reflect the gesture of Christ, Albion taking upon himself the divine act of sacrifice (see figure 52). His is the human form which most closely approximates the shape of Christ on the Cross; it is this form I have called the standing figure.

Interestingly, Blake appears to have used this figure most often for personifications of man at his spiritual extremes: Albion and Satan. Redeemed man, Albion, assumes this attitude in *Albion Rose*. Albion in *Jerusalem* 76 is the back view of the same figure. The famous inscription on the *Albion Rose* engraving emphasizes the sacrificial overtones of the image, while a demonic version appears in Satan's figure in *Job* 6. (A variant of the standing figure is Satan in the painting *Satan Calling up His Legions*.)

Blake's using the same form for such dramatically opposed states as Albion and Satan makes his point emphatically that the divinity in man can be turned to malevolence and death. Supporting evidence for the association of these figures with human divinity will be found in the apparent sources of the preliminary pencil drawings of front and back views of the standing Albion.[1] These sources have been suggested by Anthony Blunt to be Scamozzi's engraving of a proportion figure and an engraving of a bronze figure of a faun from Herculaneum (1767–71).[2] Though an image long associated with mankind, the Scamozzi figure[3] must have seemed to Blake to need the addition of lightness and grace found in the dancer-like bronze faun, which indeed the pencil sketches more closely resemble. In both figures universality and vitality are associated with outstretched arms, and these are important elements in Blake's later use of the pencilled figures. The poet who wrote of "the human form divine" and who said "all deities reside in the human breast" made his visual divine image reflect traditional icons of the human body as an ideal measure and gave it also the quality of motion. For the dance-like movement of Albion in both *Albion Rose* and *Jerusalem* 76 is the subtle but central quality which distinguishes Albion, the living human, from the passive, crucified Jesus. It expresses visually the idea of the way the divine must live in the human – that eternal life for man is a dance "of Eternal Death," continuous self-sacrifice for one's fellows. The outstretched arms of the standing form are the connecting link between Christ and Albion, which contributes to the visible expression of Albion as the "spiritual body of mankind."

The same gesture on the three other forms I have mentioned is found to have similar associations with the inherent divinity in man. In the tractates of 1788, *There Is No Natural Religion* and *All Religions Are One*, Blake used each of these forms, the knee-raised, the hovering, and the prostrate, in association with texts equating the human and divine. Accompanying Proposition VI, which, with the "Application" on the following plate, links "God," "Man," and "the Infinite," he etched a torso of a nude male with outstretched arms who looks somewhat Christ-like. The Application itself stresses the divinity of this link ("He who sees the Infinite in all things sees God") and thus, as it were, authenticates the cruciform implication of the illustration. The plate illustrating the third sentence of this proposition, "Therefore God becomes as we are, that we may be as he is," shows a prostrate figure on the ground with a halo of lines like sun-rays around its head. In *All Religions Are One*, Principle 1 (plate 4) is illustrated by an old man in the knee-raised position; the text identifies God with the Poetic Genius and imagination. In that same work, Principle 7 (plate 10) associates the hovering form, again a bearded old man, with "the True Man," the Poetic Genius.

In the last two examples, Blake represents the Poetic Genius–God–Man in the traditional artistic image of divinity in the Judeo-Christian world: both Michelangelo and Raphael show God the Creator with outstretched arms, as I have mentioned, and Jean Hagstrum sees the Raphael as a possible source of Blake's Jehovah-Urizen. Since Blake in *All Religions Are One* specifically mentioned "The Jewish & Christian Testaments" and calls them "an original derivation from the Poetic Genius" (Principle 6), the image of the patriarchal creator conventional to Western art is a natural association for him to make. The aspect of divinity most suggested by the outstretched arms of the knee-raised and hovering forms, then, is not so much sacrifice as creativity.

Because of these associations, the second or knee-raised form can perhaps be said to suggest at best God-in-man, the Poetic Genius, and at worst, fallen man's idea of God as authority. Poetic genius is implied in the figure of an old man with raised knee in *All Religions Are One*, plate 4; the similar figure of *America* 8 represents Urizen, man's perversion of his poetic genius into authority (figure 50). In the *Job* engravings this form represents one of Job's ideas of God (plate 14, *When the Morning Stars Sang Together*). In the Dante engravings the same form, with some demonic refinements, appears as *The Angry God of this World* (plate 3). Some variations of this pose appear to have similar connotations. A figure very like *America* 8 is used in *Urizen* 5, where a bearded old man holds open with outstretched arms a book which resembles the stone tablets of law (compare *Milton* 15). And a seated, bearded old man with one arm outstretched holds the wings of a youth in one hand and clips them with the other in *The Gates of Paradise* 11.[4]

There is one important instance, however, where the raised-knee form is not an old man but a young one, and since both versions occur within two plates of each other in *America*, the relation between them becomes worth examining. We have seen already that this is the stance of the Poetic Genius. Blake had written that the Poetic Genius was "everywhere call'd the Spirit of Prophecy," and *The Marriage of Heaven and Hell*, plate 24, relates outstretched arms with this faculty. At the point where Hell (that is, the free imaginative realm) and Heaven become "married," the angel "stretched out his arms," embraced the fire, was consumed,

53 Blake, *America*, plate 10

Thus wept the Angel voice & as he wept the terrible blasts
Of trumpets, blew a loud alarm across the Atlantic deep.
No trumpets answer; no reply of clarions or of fifes,
Silent the Colonies remain and refuse the loud alarm.

On those vast shady hills between America & Albions shore;
Now barr'd out by the Atlantic sea: call'd Atlantean hills:
Because from their bright summits you may pass to the Golden world
An ancient palace, archetype of mighty Emperies,
Rears its immortal pinnacles, built in the forest of God
By Ariston the king of beauty for his stolen bride.

Here on their magic seats the thirteen Angels sat perturb'd
For clouds from the Atlantic hover o'er the solemn roof.

and arose as a prophet (Elijah). Gleckner points out that in terms of the conclusion of *MHH* it is Orc, the "newborn terror," who arises,[5] and it is consistent with this idea to note that plate 10 of *America* shows a young man usually regarded as Orc surrounded by flames with his arms outstretched (see figure 53). When, turning the pages, we see that the young man's stance is quite like that of the old man (except that his left knee is raised rather than his right, making him a mirror image), we are invited to see the relationship between them. Also, beneath the image of Urizen on plate 8 the text demands that we hear the voice of Orc: "The terror answered: I am Orc, wreath'd round the accursed tree." The possibilities of their relationship hinge on the fact that both figures make the gesture associated with the Poetic Genius. In Urizen, the Poetic Genius has become part of a repressive system, the spiritual form of Albion's guardian prince, symbol of authority and restraint. His mirror image on plate 10 reflects his other self, the imaginative power of creative desire, the spirit of rebellion. Orc's pose mocks Urizen, for they are adversaries, but it also links them. Blake's Orc-Urizen myth underlies all the Lambeth books, and significantly, in *America*, the first of the prophecies, these designs provide a key to it.

The dynamic nature of these Blakean forms and the subtle way in which outstretched arms bring associations of divinity to each pose is further evident in the third design involving this gesture, the hovering figure. Because this form frequently hovers *over* someone, it develops, I believe, connotations of divinity separated in some way from the whole man or human form. The divine quality is thus in danger of being lost or becoming a Spectre, as its batwinged variations suggest. The hovering bearded man in *All Religions Are One*, plate 10, may illustrate "the True Man" (as I have suggested), but in his next appearance, in *MHH* 11, the text concerns the separation or abstraction of divine from human and how "men forgot that All deities reside in the human breast." Beneath "deities" is drawn the hovering figure, in a cloud; beneath "human breast" is a small human form, in darkness; they are about an arm's length from each other. In a more menacing aspect the hovering old man appears on the title-page of *Visions of the Daughters of Albion*, as Death in *The Lazar House* (watercolour, 1795), and as a wielder of vipers in *Christ's Troubled Dream* (*Paradise Regained*).[6]

A similar but female hovering form appears in *MHH* 14 and *VDA* 8, in each instance suggesting separation and potential but unfulfilled creativity. The first of these may be taken to show the process of change, the consuming flames of creation producing an infinite and holy state, the soul hovering over and awaiting union with the body, as the text suggests. Here the hovering figure, though still separated from the human form below it, could suggest a creative state. In the final plate of *VDA*, however, the female form in this pose, Oothoon hovering in the sky above the Daughters of Albion, is a sad and ironic echo of the hovering bearded form menacing her on the title-page, a form whose wings, rather than arms, are outstretched. What seems to be suggested is that Oothoon's failure to become one with Theotormon has made her an image of the very forces she was trying to overcome.

Although I am tempted to suggest that after *MHH* no hovering figure could mean completely good news because of these associations of separation, the potentially demonic aspect of this form is made obvious when it appears as a hovering batwinged creature (for example, in *Jerusalem* 6 and 37, and in *Gates of Paradise* tailpiece). Blake's colour print *Satan Exulting over Eve* shows Satan in a related variant of the hovering pose, with outstretched arms and batwings, over a serpent-wrapped Eve. It is important to note that batwinged creatures hover over corpse forms (that is, forms posed with arms tight at sides), but eagles or eagle-winged figures hover over cruciform prostrate forms (*America* 13, top; *VDA*; *Milton* 42). The eagle-winged Elohim in *Elohim Creating Adam* suggests the creative force behind the act of separation, while the worm-wrapped cruciform Adam retains the image of his potential divinity. (It may be suggested that the bat is the demonic aspect of the eagle, another image for two sides of a creative impulse.)

Satan and Elohim are *variations* of the hovering pose that I have called a recurring form; they are not "head-and-arms-only" designs. Yet hovering forms like them, whole hovering bodies seen at various angles, are also familiar Blakean images: *Job* 11, *With Dreams upon my bed thou scarest me; Job* 13, *Then the Lord answered Job out of the whirlwind; Job* 20 (hoverers in the background); *Jerusalem* 35; *David Delivered out of Many Waters*; *The*

54 Michelangelo, *The Creation of Adam*, detail of hand of God

Good and Evil Angels Struggling for Possession of a Child; and the same figures in MHH 4. The one feature that all these have in common is outstretched arms; all seem to generate associations that concern the separation of divine from human.

Discussion of the hovering forms has introduced us to some of the figures they hover over, so most examples of the fourth extended-arm form – the prostrate figure – have already been cited. (Because it is lying on the ground, this form is viewed from the side, and strictly speaking only one arm can be seen extended. It should be distinguished from the corpse image, whose arm is close to its side.) While this pose reminds us of the potential for regeneration, especially in its first use in *There Is No Natural Religion*, the connotations of mortality are usually uppermost, for Blake often draws it on a bier-like stone just above water or winds a serpent about the figure. Thus, at best, the form may connote Generation – or perhaps, in the case of *Milton* 42, the married peace of the state of Beulah – and at worst the Fall, a spiritual death, Adam in *Elohim Creating Adam*. This, I think, is what the serpent-wrapped extended-arm figure means when it is not, strictly speaking, prostrate. *Urizen* 6 uses the symbol of a serpent-wrapped cruciform figure, probably man falling upside-down into material existence. Blake also drew an illustration for Young's *Night Thoughts* which uses a serpent-wrapped semi-prostrate man with outstretched arms as a symbol of spiritual death in the material world.[7]

Each of the four basic outstretched-arm forms can be seen then to suggest various aspects of divinity, and within each form either the benevolent or the malevolent aspects of the divine creative impulses may be connoted. As we can see, there are details – like the presence of the serpent – which help to contextualize the forms so that the variations or additional facets of meaning become clear. In this respect, subtly differing hand positions can modify the meanings of the outstretched arms, like signals helping us to experience the designs with greater delicacy.[8]

For example, the hands of the figure in the sketched and in the engraved *Albion Rose* are turned upwards, palms out; the palms of the figure in *There Is No Natural Religion* are turned forwards; the hands of the old man with raised knee in ARO and *America* 8 are inclined downwards – until the figure is used in its final engraved form in *Job*, where the hand position changes to the creative fingers of Michelangelo's God (see figure 54). The hands of God in *Elohim Creating Adam* are sloping downwards, while those of Adam himself, whose arms are more specifically in the Latin-cross position, are turned forwards. In *Songs of Innocence*, any of the figures, from cherubs to children whose arms are outstretched to express delight, energy, or inspiration, appear to have their hands inclined upwards: see *The Echoing Green* and *The Blossom*.

This detail becomes more consistent as Blake's art develops, as we noted in chapter 1. Hand positions may not have been a deliberate

55 Blake, *When the Morning Stars Sang Together*, watercolour of *Job*, plate 14

56 Blake, *Job*, plate 14

57 Blake, *Job*, plate 20

58 Blake, *Milton*, plate 29 (A)

59 Blake, *Milton*, plate 33 (A)

symbol in their earliest use, in the form of the Poetic Genius, but certainly during the Lambeth period the position of the hands of a figure with outstretched arms seems decidedly a symbol, especially when the figure is a bearded old man. In *MHH, America* 8, and *Urizen* 28, for example, the dropping, downturned hands suggest the enfeebled or misdirected creativity of the God of this world.

The use of the hand detail to modify the meaning of a form can be observed in the *Job* designs. In the watercolour for plate 14 the hands of Jehovah droop (see figure 55); yet when Blake engraved the design, he gave the right hand "creative" fingers (see figure 56) and opened the fingers of the left hand as well. This change more graphically suggests the awakened vision of Job. Job is himself shown in the outstretched-arm attitude with the creative-hand position for both hands in the engraved plate 20 (see figure 57), where he is re-creating his experiences for his daughters. The overall form of plate 14 is still an image of fallen man's idea of God, the authoritarian God of the state of Experience, but that form at its best. As Job realizes his idea of God in himself, his gestures become like Jehovah's.

It may be argued, of course, that if Blake had been consistently using this creative-hand position symbolically, he would have used it at first, in the watercolour for plate 14. My suggestion is that this case is rather like revisions in a poem. The right gesture, like the right word, alters or modifies a theme; the artist experiments until he is satisfied.

The pattern of using a receptive palms-up or -outward position on Adam, Albion, or Christ figures was a usual practice of Blake's, as even a cursory examination of designs will reveal (for example, in *Jerusalem* 76 or in the *Paradise Lost* series). In *Milton* the upturned hand is found in two important places; in the two plates which represent Robert and William Blake receiving the divine spirit, the figures are shown leaning back with arms outstretched, palms turned up (figures 58 and 59).

Similarly, downturned hands are used to powerful effect in, for example, *The Lazar House*, where the hovering figure of Death (as the bearded old man) has his palms turned down, or in the figure of the evil angel in *The Good & Evil Angels Struggling for Possession of a Child*. The downturned hands on the hovering variant of the outstretched-arms form are to be seen in Blake's *Paradise Lost* series, plate 4, *Satan's and Raphael's Entries into Paradise*, where once again the figure seems to represent the God of the fallen world, the Hebraic God of Milton's *Paradise Lost*. The association of the downturned hand with creativity turned to rationalism and abstraction can be seen vividly in Blake's colour print *Newton*, where the left hand of Newton, sloping downwards, holds the triangular compasses. The detail of the downturned hand may, then, bear a message in regard to the Orc figure of plate 10 of *America*. This form has the same downturned hands as the Urizen figure of plate 8: perhaps Orc here may not be a completely regenerated figure – indeed,

60 Blake, *The Great Red Dragon and the Woman Clothed with the Sun: The Devil Is Come Down*

as a representative of the cycle of time he could hardly be the completely redeemed man. Blake himself drew attention to the importance of such details in his art when he wrote, "I intreat then that the Spectator will attend to the Hands & Feet ... they are all descriptive of Character & not a line is drawn without intention & that most discriminate and particular" (E 560).

Taking into consideration the four basic outstretched-arm images and the significant related details that we have been discussing, it can be suggested that these four forms may approximate mental states. There appears to be a progression from the prostrate form to the standing: implied is a movement from the *separation* of human and divine suggested by hovering and prostrate forms, through *creation* (of the mortal and finite), as suggested by the Jehovah-Urizen associations of the knee-raised form, to divine sacrifice or *union* of man and divine in the standing form. And because the standing figure can be either of the extreme states, Albion or Satan, this form most vividly expresses the dynamic potential of all these states in one man.

One design which uses many of the symbols I have been discussing is the watercolour *The Great Red Dragon and the Woman Clothed with the Sun* (see figure 60). The hovering figure is here taken to its ultimate satanic form, encompassing batwings, serpent tail, and outstretched arms with downturned hands. According to Revelation the dragon is "that old serpent, called the Devil, and Satan, which deceiveth the whole world" (Rev. 12:9). The woman clothed with the sun and given the wings of an eagle represents the good *in nature* (she sits on a crescent moon), which the dragon is trying to vanquish; Blake indicates this also by her outstretched arms, her upturned hands, and her position on a stone in the sea rather reminiscent of Urizen in *America* 8. The natural world of sun, moon, stone, and sea are her province, as they are his. Blake tells us how he reads the passage in Revelation, however, by the way in which the positions of woman and dragon reflect each other: these are two aspects of the same psyche, as powerful an image of the demonic and regenerative impulses of fallen man as he ever painted.

The symbolic gesture of outstretched arms, then, can be associated consistently with the main themes of Blake's work: the essential divinity of man, his capacity for regeneration, his error in turning the divine creativity into mental tyranny or selfhood. The importance of the four attitudes which repeatedly represent these ideas in Blake's art may remind us of his exclamation, "What kind of Intellects must he have who sees only the Colours of things & not the Forms of Things" ("Public Address," E 578). The outstretched-arms motif, perhaps the most evident of several of Blake's repeated visual images, should not then be ignored or dismissed as a technical weakness; it is a symbol as powerful as any verbal symbol and essential to that union of sight and sound, that reintegration of the senses which Blake strove to achieve in all his work.

OTHER VARIATIONS OF THE OUTSTRETCHED ARMS

Supine or prone figures, flat on the ground, viewed head-on (*A Poison Tree*, *Gates of Paradise* 7, *America* title-page)
This appears to mean death by violence, spiritual or physical murder. The most conclusive proofs of this meaning are in the designs for *Night Thoughts*, where there are several uses of this image connected with texts of violence. For example, a design for Night VIII (*NT* 413) shows a strangled figure in this position; in Night IX a Urizenic figure in this position has an arrow sticking out of his chest, associated with the lines: "He falls on his own Scythe; nor falls alone; / His greatest Foe falls with him, Time, and He / Who murder'd all Time's offspring, Death, expire" (*NT* 435). However, the text of *The Gates of Paradise* for plate 7 also suggests murder. There appears to be no regenerative use made of this form: when the opposite state is to be indicated, the upright-standing figure is used.

Striding figures, arms outstretched (*Urizen* 3; *MHH* 3; *Jerusalem* 26)
This seems to be an image of either creative or demonic energy. It is often associated with flames. E.J. Rose has written interestingly of *Jerusalem* 26 in "Blake's Hand" (see note 8).

The outstretched arms at oblique angle (*Jerusalem* 99; angels in *Job* 14, *When the Morning Stars* ...; Satan in *Satan Calling up His Legions*; *Gates of Paradise* 7; *VDA* title-page; *Thel* title-page)
This would seem to be a welcoming or a worshipping gesture; a demonic aspect of the symbol is fear or flight (see the last three examples above).

The outstretched arms forward (Elohim in *Elohim Creating Adam*; the accusers in *Job* 10; God in *Job* 17; the man in the Arlington Court picture; *Jerusalem* 93)
This gesture appears to signify casting a spell or creating an error or a self-image. The regenerative aspect of the symbol is blessing (*Job* 17). The position of the fingers is an important detail of this gesture: they are usually "creative."

FOUR

Figures of Despair

There is another complex of figures which recurs often enough in Blake's designs that we may assume it is an important component of his symbolic language based on the human form. One of these recurring images is a hunched figure with drawn-up knees, viewed from the front, as in *Jerusalem*, plate 37 (figure 62). This figure and its related form, the bent-over, kneeling figure, as in *America* 16 and *Job* 6 (figures 61 and 63), are recognized by most readers to be Blake's primary visual symbols for mankind in the state of despair. Two other images are important to this complex: the head-clutching, falling figure, as in *Urizen* 6 (figure 64), and the prostrate adult figure with arms close to its side, exemplified by Job in *Job* 6.[1] An exploration of Blake's use of these four forms and their variations may help to reinforce our understanding of Blake's subtle perceptions of one of mankind's most devastating emotions.

Although we may think of Blake as a supremely energetic and cheerful man, that he wrestled with despair many times in his life is evident to the reader of his works and letters. It is very moving to read the simple entry in his notebook: "Tuesday, Jan^{ry} 20, 1807, between Two and Seven in the Evening – Despair." Despair is one of the names given to the Spectre in *Jerusalem*, and it is this connection between the concept of the Spectre and the concept of despair in Blake's work which I hope this chapter will illuminate. Blake's meaning for both has many facets, yet the destructive aspect of the power of reason, which is essentially the Spectre, is one of the basic components of despair:

> This is the Spectre of Man: the Holy Reasoning Power
> And in its Holiness is closed the Abomination of Desolation
> (*J* 10: 15–16; E 153).

Not only desolation but the traditional medieval suicidal implications of despair are expressed by the Spectre's speech in *Jerusalem*, chapter 1:

61 Blake, *America*, plate 16

62 Blake, *Jerusalem*, plate 37

O that I could cease to be! Despair! I am Despair
Created to be the great example of horror & agony: also my
Prayer is vain I called for compassion: compassion mockd
Mercy & pity threw the grave stone over me & with lead
And iron, bound it over me forever: Life lives on my
Consuming: & the Almighty hath made me his Contrary
To be all evil, all reversed & for ever dead: knowing
And seeing life, yet living not; how can I then behold
And not tremble; how can I be beheld & not abhorrd? (*J* 10: 51–9; E 154)

This passage is a reflection of medieval theological ideas of despair – *wanhope*, despair of the mercy of God – found most clearly expressed in Chaucer's parson's account of *accidie*, or sloth:

Now comth wanhope, that is despair of the mercy of God, that comth somtyme of to muche outrageous sorwe, and somtyme of to muche drede, ymaginynge that he hath doon so muche synne that it wol nat availlen hym ...

The attributes which Blake gives to the Spectres of the Zoas in *Jerusalem* appear to be closely based on the description in *The Parson's Tale* of accidie, which makes man a "hevy, thoghtful, and wraw." Doubt, "cooldnesse," "sompnolence," "ydelnesse," and sorrow, which "wereth to the deeth of the soule and the body also," are all succinctly described by Blake as the behaviour of the Zoas when they turn against Albion and become Spectres:

They saw their Wheels rising up poisonous against Albion
Urizen, cold & scientific; Luvah, pitying & weeping
Tharmas, indolent & sullen: Urthona, doubting & despairing
Victims to one another & dreadfully plotting against each other
To prevent Albion walking about in the Four Complexions.
(*J* 38: 1–5; E 184)

This passage is reiterated with further emphasis on accidie or "deadly stupor":

And the Four Zoas are Urizen & Luvah & Tharmas & Urthona
In opposition deadly, and their Wheels in poisonous
And deadly stupor turn'd against each other loud & fierce
Entering into the Reasoning Power, forsaking Imagination
They became Spectres; & their Human Bodies were reposed
In Beulah, by the Daughters of Beulah with tears & lamentations
(*J* 74: 4–9; E 229).

This accidie or accidia, the deadly sin which is despair,[2] is part of what happens to Albion and may indeed be the "deadly Sleep" that the Four-fold Man has fallen into. This is certainly suggested by the design of *Jerusalem* 37 (which has been called Humanity Asleep),[3] in which Blake explicitly tells us by the words on the scroll that the form represents man in his Spectre's power:

> Each Man is in his Spectre's power
> Until the arrival of that hour

63 Blake, *Job*, plate 6

When his Humanity awake
And cast his Spectre into the Lake.

Clearly, before the full implications of this design can be realized, it is necessary to explore further what the "power" of the Spectre implies.[4]

Blake would have been well acquainted with the concept of despair as it was treated not only in Chaucer but in other literature and art from medieval times to his own. It was a subject which "profoundly affected the Medieval imagination, the sin against the Holy Ghost, the sin of sins, in that it tempted to self-destruction and thereby shut off every hope of

64 Blake, *The Book of Urizen*, plate 6

repentance and salvation."[5] Dante, whose work Blake was illustrating at the time of his death, had made despair, the abandonment of hope, "the very condition of entrance into Hell."[6] Blake translated Dante's inscription ("lasciate ogni speranza, voi ch'entrate") literally as "Leave every hope you who in enter" when he pencilled it in over the gate in his drawing *The Inscription over the Gate*. Personifications of despair and the other cardinal sins were common in Middle English poets such as Lydgate, Langland, and Gower, and the tradition flourished in English fifteenth-century literature (Dunbar, Hawes), eventually crowned by Spenser's *Faerie Queene*, with its description of the Cave of Despair and the procession of the Sins.[7] Blake attempted something in this tradition in his rather obscure fragment "Then She Bore Pale Desire." Richard Burton, whose *Anatomy of Melancholy* culminated a series of English writings on melancholy, devoted the last six subsections to a discussion of the sin of despair. However, it was the figures of Despair as personified in Spenser and Bunyan which stimulated Blake's imagination, as I will later indicate, and his designs for Milton's *L'Allegro* and *Il Penseroso* show him well aware of the tradition as it was adapted by that poet. There is an interesting similarity to Blake's designs *Milton Led by Melancholy* (illustration to *L'Allegro* reproduced in Butlin, plate 543) and *The Wood of the Self-Murderers: the Harpies and the Suicides* (illustration to *The Divine Comedy*, Roe 24). In both a poet is about to be led into a wood where unhappy spirits animate the trees, the experience being part of a process which leads to the ultimate regeneration of the poet. Melancholy is, of course, allied to despair (there are several Despair figures in Blake's Milton designs), and the implication that sorrow may be turned to the good of man, that it is not an end in itself, is a message that Blake shares with Milton and projects in both design and poetry.

The relation between the concepts of melancholy and despair, and the iconographic tradition behind them, is, of course, extremely complex and has been traced in the monumental study by R. Klibansky, F. Saxl, and E. Panofsky, *Saturn and Melancholy*. They have demonstrated that by the late Middle Ages the notions of melancholy and accidia were equated and that by Milton's time melancholy had indeed become an intellectual force or tutelary spirit. The Miltonic Penseroso "combined all the aspects of the melancholic: the ecstatic and the contemplative, the silent and Saturnine no less than the musical and Apollonian, the gloomy prophet and the idyllic lover of nature, and welded their manifoldness into a unified picture, mild on the whole rather than menacing."[8] Blake seems to have understood *Il Penseroso* in much this way, for his representation of Milton in *Milton and His Mossy Cell* follows an iconographic tradition for figures of melancholia, that is, a seated, pensive figure, often viewed from the front.[9] Blake would have known this tradition from Michelangelo, Cesare Ripa's *Iconologia*, and Dürer's *Melencholia I*, and it is this tradition to which I believe all of his hunched Despair figures are related.[10] Blake shows Milton seated in a cave or cell, surrounded by various spirits of nature, flowers, and stars, with his arms outstretched in a gesture of creativity, this variation indicating the possible regenerative aspect of melancholy.[11] Blake's involvement with the concepts of melancholy and despair as they were treated by eighteenth-century writers who further refined and extended these notions is, of course, evident in his illustrations of Gray's poetry and especially in his more than five hundred designs for Young's *Night Thoughts*. In the *Night Thoughts* designs, the hunched figure is consistently used to represent despair or deep sorrow.[12]

In his own poetry, Blake came to associate despair with a reasoning power cut off from imagination (*J* 74: 10–13) and with desolation, much as St Thomas Aquinas had defined accidia as "tristitia de spirituali bono," the sorrow about or the aversion man feels against his spiritual good[13] (taking the spiritual good, in Blake's terms, to be imagination).

Spenser had demonstrated a similar self-destructive state in the apparently reasonable argument for suicide that Despair put to the Redcrosse Knight (*Faerie Queene*, canto IX). Thus for Blake the Spectre is both the "Reasoning Power in Man" and the despair which such reasoning brings about.[14]

Now the source of accidia as well as of all the other deadly sins is pride. The false pride of mankind which both Swift and Pope rail against comes under attack from Blake too, who early uses the same weapons of satire and parody (as in *An Island in the Moon* and *MHH*) but with the added advantage of being able to use his graver to produce other dimensions of social comment. Like Swift and Pope, Blake's work intensifies in tone as his vision encompasses man's enormous vanity and selfishness, which he calls the Selfhood, the very basic difference being that Blake saw that the Selfhood was "worshipd as God by the Mighty Ones of the Earth" (*J* 29: 33; the Selfhood is the Spectre that Blake's Milton recognizes as Satan and himself – "I in my Selfhood am that Satan: I am that Evil One! / He is my Spectre!").[15] The Spectres of the Zoas possess this pride also:

> The Four Zoas rush around on all sides in dire ruin
> Furious in pride of Selfhood the terrible Spectres of Albion
> Rear their dark Rocks among the Stars of God: stupendous
> Works! (*J* 58: 47–50; E 208)

This Satanic activity and Milton's explicit reference recall the words of the Spectres' "Despair" speech quoted previously, "the Almighty hath made me his Contrary / To be all evil." We should therefore expect to find designs in which the Spectre is drawn as Satan (the traditional archetype of pride) in conjunction with huddled, falling, and prostrate Despair forms, and this is indeed the case, as in *Job* 6 and the design *Satan Calling Up His Legions*, to name only two.[16]

There is a relation then between the Spectre, despair, and pride in

Blake's work which bears examining, for to reveal the paradoxes of these concepts appears to be the purpose of much of his poetry and painting. Thus, in *MHH*, "Milton is of the Devil's party without knowing it," "The pride of the peacock is the glory of God," and a whole dualistic world-view is called into question. The Spectre Selfhood must be "put off & annihilated alway" (*Milton* 40: 36), but in the process a humanizing creative energy is released, as Blake describes in the struggles of Milton and Los.

In Blake's art, it is always necessary to distinguish between representations of man in the power of the Spectre, and thus in the state of despair, and representations of the Spectre itself. Blake appears careful to make these distinctions both visually and verbally. The individuals taken over by Spectres are blameless:

> ... Iniquity must be imputed only
> To the state they are enterd into that they may be deliverd:
> Satan is the State of Death & not a Human existence ...
> Learn therefore ... to distinguish the Eternal Human ...
> From those States or Worlds in which the Spirit travels
> (*J* 49: 65–74; E 199).

The visual images for the Spectre include recognizable satanic figures, beasts, batwinged hovering forms, and serpent-dragon forms. It is significant that Blake's roster of Spectre images follows, to a surprising extent, the traditional iconographic representation of pride when it is symbolized by animals in literature or art. The list, compiled by Bloomfield, includes the lion, peacock, eagle, horse, bull, elephant, unicorn, cuckoo, basilisk, dromedary, ram, and leviathan.[17]

The links between the state of despair, the Spectres, and the deadly sins of accidia and pride which I have been tracing can be extended to include the rest of the cardinal sins: envy, lust, gluttony, avarice, and wrath. Traditionally they are all aspects of despair[18] and are reflected in the Spectre's behaviour. As I have indicated, Blake appears well aware of religious tradition regarding the seven deadly sins, which in his poetry are sometimes called spiritual diseases[19]: "The Seven diseases of the Soul / Settled around Albion" (*J* 19: 27). The sins are the creation of Satan in *Milton* (9: 20) and are thus linked to the Spectre Selfhood much as theology links them to pride. Basically the sins to Blake are products of frustrated desire and are not in themselves evil. In *The Book of Los* he writes of a time when

> ... none impure were deem'd:
> Not Eyeless Covet,
> Nor thin-lip'd Envy,
> Nor Bristled Wrath,
> Nor Curled Wantonness;

But Covet was poured full,
Envy fed with fat of lambs,
Wrath with lions gore,
Wantonness lull'd to sleep
With the virgin's lute
Or sated with her love. (E 90)

Blake had connected despair with frustrated desire in *There Is No Natural Religion*: "If any could desire what he is incapable of possessing, despair must be his eternal lot" (plate VIb). Under the category of frustrated desire it is possible to place envy, lust, gluttony, and avarice and to see them all embodied in this speech of the Spectre of Urthona:

Thou knowest that the Spectre is in Every Man insane brutish
Deformd that I am thus a ravening devouring lust continually
Craving & devouring ... (*FZ* VII: 84; E 360)

It would be possible to demonstrate at much greater length that each of the fallen Zoas (with their Emanations) experience most of the sins at one time or another. The example of Tharmas will serve as an indication.

The Spectre of Tharmas appears early in *The Four Zoas* as a golden, winged human form, "... rapturous in fury / Glorying in his own eyes / Exalted in terrific Pride." This wrath and pride are followed by lust for his Emanation ("burning anguish"). Enion herself experiences envy ("jealous fear") of Enitharmon and commits murder. Eventually Tharmas becomes the very embodiment of accidia, a death-wish personified:

... give me death
For death to me is better far than life. death my desire
That I in vain in various paths have sought but still I live
(*FZ* VI: 69; E 346).

Tharmas is similarly described in *Jerusalem* as "indolent and sullen." However, in his fallen aspect as the Covering Cherub Tharmas also suggests the sins of avarice and gluttony, with the repeated references to his coveting of "precious stones" and his "devouring Stomach" (*J* 89). Tharmas is further the personification of the senses of touch and taste,[20] the "Angel of the Tongue," and when by his fall he becomes "... the Vegetated Tongue, even the Devouring Tongue ... the False Tongue" (*J* 14), it is wrath which dominates his utterances. Thus, in the fall of Tharmas, the "parent Power," all the sins are suggested.[21]

Since for Blake frustrated desire is the basis of the cardinal sins, wrath is a psychologically valid result, and incidentally a reaction which an artist can depict vividly in a visual medium. When the Zoas divide, originally they divide in rage (*J* 74: 1), which is the keynote sounded by the

65 Blake, *America*, frontispiece

gures
Despair

66 Blake, illustration to *Pilgrim's Progress: Christian and Hopeful in Doubting Castle*

first line of *Vala*. Fury creates the fallen world, and the Sins assume living form in *The Book of Urizen*:

> Rage, fury, intense indignation
> In cataracts of fire blood & gall
> In whirlwinds of sulphurous smoke:
> And enormous forms of energy,
> All the seven deadly sins of the soul
> In living creations appear'd
> In the flames of eternal fury. (*BU* 5; E 72)

It is significant that the visual images which dominate *The Book of Urizen* are the falling and huddled images of despair figures.

It will not have escaped the close observer of Blake's designs that some of the variations of the hunched and falling figures, particularly those in *Urizen* (for example, plate 16 or plate 22), emanate a powerful energy which seems the contrary of accidia. Wrath, however, is the daughter-sin of despair and can be redemptive, becoming the force of Revolution, Orc, and the angry prophet, Rintrah. *America*, the first poem in which Orc plays a dominant role, begins and ends with figures of Depair, the frontispiece (figure 65) and plate 16 (figure 61), underlining for the reader the paradoxical connections between the "contraries" of energy and despair, which can imply "progression." I have written in chapter 3 that most of Blake's recurring images can have a redemptive as well as a demonic interpretation. In the case of despair figures, however, I am of the opinion that their truly redemptive form is actually a contrasting energy figure – for example, an upward-soaring rather than a falling figure, a dancing or striding figure rather than a huddled or prostrate one. Energy figures have their demonic meanings (for example, Satan in *Job* 6 is a demonic Albion of *Albion Rose*) but I have not found a despair form used to suggest a regenerated state. At their best they connote sleep, which in itself suggests a fallen state.

At this point it is necessary to recall that in *There Is No Natural Religion*, immediately after stating in plate VI that despair must be the eternal lot of the man who desires what he is incapable of possessing, Blake asserts: "The desire of Man being Infinite the possession is Infinite & himself Infinite." By this juxtaposition we know that the state of despair means the opposite of "Infinite" – that is, the closed-up world of boundaries and ratios, Urizen's world, the world of fallen nature. The repeated circular huddled representations of Los and Urizen in *The Book of Urizen* suggest that the form is emblematic for the material world.[22] Thus the despair form and the Spectre come together again in the fallen Urizen: "The Spectre is the Reasoning Power in Man; & when separated / From Imagination, and closing itself as in steel, in a Ratio / Of the Things of Memory. It thence frames Laws & Moralities / To Destroy Imagination ..." (*J* 74: 10–13; E 229). Blake's representation of the worm-mother, Tirzah, in *Gates of Paradise* 16 also indicates that fallen nature is a meaning we should attach to the huddled pose.

Here the text of the poem *To Tirzah* becomes important, for the binding of the senses in "mortal clay" is a tyranny both physical and mental, which Blake often indicates by using chains and manacles in his illustrations. In a world produced by self-enclosure, Despair becomes a jailer. Blake has graphically illustrated both the jailer dangling keys and his huddled victim in one of his illustrations to Bunyan's *Pilgrim's Progress*, *Christian and Hopeful in Doubting Castle* (figure 66). Bunyan's jailer Giant Despair is represented as a satanic Spectre form – indeed, he is a kind of rear-view version of Satan in *Job* 6. (This design should be compared to *Europe* 13, which includes the same jailer with keys disappearing up the cell stairs, and a hunched despair figure.) The giant appears again in plate 25 of the illustrations to John Bunyan's *The Pilgrim's Progress*, this time with a club. Bunyan's description of the Giant Despair is brief:

> He had a cap of steel upon his head, a breast-plate of figure girded to him, and he came out in iron shoes, with a great club in his hand.

Blake omits the cap and armour in the illustrations, but he seems to have had Bunyan's passage in mind when he described the Spectre of Urthona as an iron man:

> A spectre Vast appeard whose feet & legs with iron scaled ...
> Round his loins a girdle glowd with many colourd fires
> In his hand a knotted Club ...
> Black scales of iron arm the dread visage iron spikes instead
> Of hair shoot from his orbed scull ... (*FZ* VI: 75; E 352)

This passage amplifies the "naming" of the Spectre as Despair which we have seen in *Jerusalem* 10, and the Bunyan designs, executed late in Blake's life, indicate how consistent he was both in his use of visual images and in his care in distinguishing visually between the Spectre and the man in the Spectre's power.

Blake's imagination may have been stimulated to create the hunched-over figure as a symbol of despair not only by iconographic tradition but also by Spenser's stanzas describing "That cursed wight ... A man of hell, that calls himself Despaire ..." in book I of *The Faerie Queene*:

> That darkesome cave they enter, where they find
> That cursed man, low sitting on the ground,
> Musing full sadly in his sullein mind:
> His griesie lockes, long growen and unbound,
> Disordred hong about his shoulders round,
> And hid his face; through which his hollow eyne
> Lookt deadly dull, and stared as astound ... (canto IX, XXXV)

Two more designs using the hunched figure, each with connotations of Hell, are the Dante design *The Mission of Virgil* (Roe 3) and Blake's colour print *Hecate*. Another Dante design repeats the form with similar connotations: it is the Urizenic winged angel in *Dante and Virgil Approaching the Angel who Guards the Entrance of Purgatory*. All these forms make an interesting comparison to the winged hunched figure in the frontispiece to *America* and to a related sketch in the *Vala* manuscript of the winged Spectre of Tharmas (page 5), for they are all guardians of some kind of portal: Hell, the underworld, Purgatory for the first group and Generation for the last two, which have associations with the Covering Cherub, or "Eternal Death."[23]

Up to this point I have been referring mainly to hunched, front-view figures, which if examined more closely could be seen to range from the rather noble representation of Albion in *Jerusalem* 37 to the grotesques of *Urizen*. Blake's variations are always subtle – a head bowed or unbowed, a gesture of arm or hand, knees open or ankles crossed – and yet they are always important clues to meaning, underlining the anger or frustration or malevolence or simply the passivity which is part of the spiritual condition. In this respect, the bent-over kneeling figure, which is often a woman, connotes a slightly different aspect of despair. It is a somewhat more grief-stricken figure, which can never express wrath, for example, but radiates fear or worshipful subjection (figures 62 and 63). Blake suggests the meaning for this form in a passage in *The Four Zoas* where Albion and Vala worship the Urizenic shadow of Albion:

> Man fell upon his face prostrate before the watry shadow ...
> And Vala trembled & coverd her face, & her locks. were spread on the
> pavement (*FZ* III: 40; E 327).

The prostrated image of Mother Nature on the final plate of *America* (figure 62) seems to be an embodiment of these words and becomes in its context in the poem a kind of emblematic form of subjection to a tyranny, the Urizenic cycle of nature. These lines, of course, come from a passage which, as Damon has demonstrated, is repeated in *Jerusalem* (29: 33–83) and is closely connected with the story of *Job*, for in it Albion accepts his Shadow as God, rejects his emotional life, and is smitten by Luvah with boils:[24]

> And Luvah strove to gain dominion over the mighty Albion
> They strove together above the Body where Vala was inclos'd
> And the dark Body of Albion left prostrate upon the crystal pavement
> Coverd with boils from head to foot. the terrible smitings of Luvah
> (*FZ* III: 41; E 328).

The relation between this passage and the design of *Job* 6 is important, for it demonstrates how a picture which Blake expressed first in words could remain in his imagination for several years to take concrete form in a design. Not only the picture but the very elements of the design, the individual figures, are given visual expression in forms which he consistently used throughout his life with symbolic meanings. Blake's *Job* designs are effectively a guidebook to his symbolic forms. Each of the despair figures is found in the *Job* series – a natural enough expectation, given that Job's experience is intimately connected with that state. Two of the four forms are found in *Job* 6, the third figure being Satan, whose relation to the Spectre and despair I have already mentioned.

Job's affliction with disease is, in Blake's terms, an affliction with sin, "The seven diseases of the Soul" (*J* 19: 26). *Job* 6, therefore, is the picture of a man being sickened with spiritual diseases by his Spectre, resulting in the despair of his Emanation. The figures are all so intimately connected – Job's feet touch his knees and Satan stands on Job's body – that they are obviously all aspects of Job's psyche: this is man in his Spectre's power with a vengeance. Job's prostrate form here and in plate 11, where he is also menaced by Spectres, is a symbol of despair also. Comparable images are the prostrate figures in the colour print *The Lazar House* and the top design of *Jerusalem* 94. Some qualification is necessary here, however, for the gesture of Job's hands in both cases indicates a kind of protest (it is like the gesture of the huddled despair figure in *Europe* 13), and the other figures in the designs mentioned are contorted. These details help us to see Blake's distinctions – I have discussed in chapter 3 the prostrate cruciform figure, which has slightly different connotations of lost divinity – and when, for example, we find a prostrate figure making no gesture at all, on a bier, menaced by a batwinged Spectre, as in *Jerusalem* 33, we can assume that a nadir has been reached. I believe that there are subtle differences between Blake's use of a corpse form like *Jerusalem* 33, a prostrate cruciform figure like Adam in *Elohim Creating Adam*, and a prostrate "moving" or gesturing figure like Job. In the latter the connotations of illness and suffering are uppermost, while with the corpse the associations of spiritual death are dominant; with the cruciform figure, the capacity for regeneration is emphasized. With Blake's designs, the observer of Minute Particulars is always rewarded.

Finally, as many scholars have noticed, a consistent gesture used by Blake with despair figures is head-clutching. The early design which accompanies plate VI of *There Is No Natural Religion*, whose words define despair as frustrated desire, shows a seated figure clutching his head. This gesture is often used in *Urizen*, and frequently with falling figures. Blake described such falling figures as "attitudes of Despair and Horror" (*VLJ*, E 557). Of the same figures he has also written that they are "attitudes of contention representing various States of Misery, which alas, every one on Earth is liable to enter into, & against which we should all watch."[25]

The frequency with which the serpent is drawn wound about or associated with these falling figures emphasizes the relation of the idea of the Fall into mortality or Generation, and despair. The serpent is a Spectre form analogous to Satan, and Blake's words, "Man is born a Spectre or Satan" (*J* 52), are another way of saying that we are all in our Spectre's power in the fallen world. The form of Albion in *Jerusalem* 37 tells us the same thing, and one other detail also gives us the same message: the words on the scroll saying "Each Man is in his Spectre's Power ..." are in reversed script, or mirror writing. The reflecting agent thus becomes the reader: we are all mirror images of Albion.

But, of course, to concentrate on figures of despair is not really being fair to Blake, for his whole message concerns the awakening of Albion, the way in which the Spectre must be made to work for man in the fallen world and embraced as a brother. Even the "diseases" of the seven deadly sins are curable by fortitude and forgiveness and would presumably return to their eternal state of spiritual energy.[26] This awakening is described in Blake's letter to Thomas Butts (22 November 1802) in terms of emerging into light from darkness (significantly, in Blake's poetry the adjective which most often collocates with the word *despair* is the word *dark*):

> And now let me finish with assuring you that Tho I have been very unhappy I am so no longer I am again Emerged into the light of Day I still & shall to Eternity Embrace Christianity and Adore him who is the Express image of God but I have traveld thro Perils & Darkness not unlike a Champion I have Conquerd and shall still Go on Conquering Nothing can withstand the fury of my Course among the Stars of God & in the Abysses of the Accuser My Enthusiasm is still what it was only Enlarged and confirmd (E 720).

At this point we realize that the spiritual form of such a man is no longer huddled in self-enclosure or prostrated by emotions but standing upright, like the figure of Albion in his dialogue with Christ (*J* 76), ready to embrace all the world.

IVE

Figures of Energy: The Leap

Despair and desire are antithetical ideas in Blake's work: "If any could desire what he is incapable of possessing, despair must be his eternal lot" *TNR* b, 1788). In the last chapter I discussed visual forms of despair in Blake's art, the huddled, falling shapes. Visual symbols of desire have the opposite dynamic – they are upward-soaring, open, flying. They are meant to suggest infinite capacity and sometimes godliness, for as Blake saw it: "The desire of Man being Infinite, the possession is Infinite, & himself Infinite" (*TNR* b, 1788). Another term closely related to Blake's *desire* is *energy*, the very opposite of the lassitude of despair; Blake's figures of energy and figures of desire are often the same, as will be demonstrated in this chapter.

The concept of energy in Blake's work has been admirably traced by Morton Paley;[1] what I demonstrate here is one way in which Blake visualizes the idea in its aspect of motion. I am again interested in the process by which an idea takes visual form and the way in which that form in its repeated use conveys meaning.

Blake introduces his concept of energy early, in *The Marriage of Heaven and Hell* (begun in 1790). From the beginning it is associated with more than ordinary images of motion. In plate 3, the metaphor implied and the meaning of the words are consistent: contraries "spring." Reason and Energy are contraries, like attraction and repulsion, love and hate; without them is no *progression*. "Evil is the active *springing* from Energy" (emphasis added). The image of an upward-leaping figure is created by the words, and the idea is further crystallized as a human figure when we read in plate 4: "Energy is the only life and is from the Body and Reason is the bound or outward circumference of Energy." This implies that Reason provides the outline or boundary of a body, the "wirey bounding line" so important to Blake's idea of good art. These contraries work together, then, to create form. Reason in a very graphic way contains (holds in) Energy. Energy can be Eternal Delight because Reason allows us to discern it. The negative side of this concept is, of course, that the binding of Energy can suppress it too far and its domination by Reason drive it into demonic channels. *MHH* shows us that these channels too can be liberating.

What we soon realize, however, is that energy takes many forms in Blake's work. It is the power which liberates, becoming personified in Blake's early works as Orc, the revolutionary spirit. It is Blake's essential element for the sublime: power, terror, wrath, infinity are all associated with energy in Blake's writing and designs. It is a quality possessed uniquely by Blake's idea of Christ. My intention here is to approach Blake's concept through selected designs, examining figures which clarify aspects of psychic rather than physical energy, for Blake makes such distinctions often through his pictures. I examine leaping and soaring figures in this chapter – gravity-free figures. In my next chapter I examine gravity-bound forms, the dancing figures.

In Blake's language of visual symbols, a singularly beautiful attitude appears to be consistently used to represent psychic energy. It is the flying or leaping human form, springing upwards with one leg bent and one arm reaching up or sideways. The figure is nearly always drawn

67 Blake, *Visions of the Daughters of Albion*, "The Argument"

back-view and is often but not always a female. The curve of hip or bend of torso may be more accentuated in some designs than in others, and the figure may spring from either the right or left leg, but the basic pattern of the image is readily identifiable. Two examples of the form

68 Blake, *Europe*, plate 9

69 Blake, illustration to Thomas Gray's *Ode on the Spring*, title-page

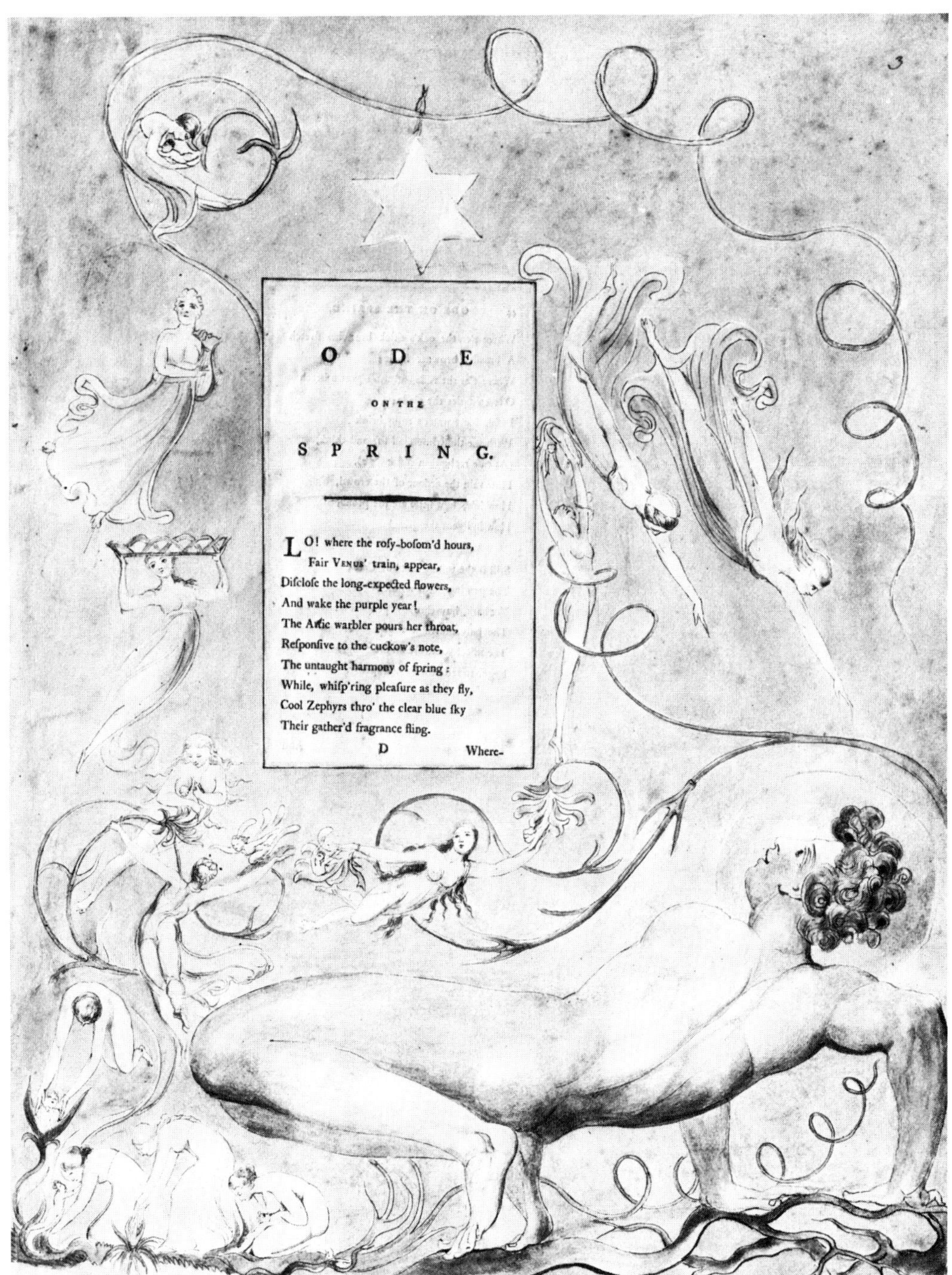

are found in *VDA* ("The Argument") and *Europe* 9 (figures 67 and 68). Other examples occur on the title-page of *America*, in *Vala*, pages 3 and 139, and in *Jerusalem* 46. In the *Night Thoughts* designs these figures appear very frequently and are used by Blake to personify what Young writes of as "joys" and sometimes "wishes."[2] What seems clear is that this leaping or rising figure is meant to represent something *non-corporeal*: one design which indicates this meaning is *Night Thoughts* 114 (figure 13), which shows a female figure dropping a mask, called a "mask of flesh" in the text. The form here is intended to represent an essence, a pure idea.

Again, this is the meaning conveyed by the design and text of the Argument of *VDA*, where the graceful leaping figure is the essence of Leutha's flower, the human form of the flower, and therefore the human image of the desire. This means of humanizing nature is again employed in Blake's illustration to the title-page of Thomas Gray's *Ode on the Spring* (figure 69), where the same figure appears. Blake uses this leaping figure also to humanize another aspect of vegetable nature, time. In the *Night Thoughts* designs, there are at least two examples of the form representing a *moment* (*NT* 19 and 155; see figures 70 and 71).

In my early essay "Blake's Use of Gesture" I was of the opinion that the leaping figure represents both spiritual and physical energy. I am now of the opinion that this attitude is intended to suggest the psychic rather than the physical in pictures where it is possible to compare a corporeal and non-corporeal form (as in *VDA* Argument or on the title-page of *America*). It is of course possible to say that all of Blake's illustrations are depictions of non-corporeal states – personifications and allegorical figures are, after all, psychic states. But I think we can discern different orders of visual allegory: for example, Job, his wife, the accusers, other Biblical personages in Blake's designs, Milton, and Albion, all have a basic physical existence which we grant. The inhabitants of a non-corporeal realm include depictions of nature humanized and elemental forces like demons or angels. The figure of Christ, which partakes of both realms, is a special case which I discuss later in the chapter.

As the visual form of a *wish*, the leaping figure appears frequently in the *Night Thoughts*, explicitly illustrated, as in 392, where the form is winged to represent the text "Thy fickle wish is ever on the Wing." (On the verso pages of Night VI (*NT* 217) and Night VII, title-page (*NT* 267), a variation of the design, with the legs horizontal, expresses a rush of motion or propulsion; see figure 72.) Again, in Blake's illustrations to the poems of Gray, we see the form twice illustrating muses (*The Progress of Poesy*, plates 8 and 12; see figures 73 and 74). Once more, this is a specific, creative, non-corporeal, self-propelled kind of energy.

In *Jerusalem*, Blake still uses the leaping figure with associations of creative desire and the essential energies of nature. In *Jerusalem* 46 (figure 75) the suggestion of aspiration clings to the leaping form of the

70 Blake, illustration to Edward Young's *Night Thoughts* 19

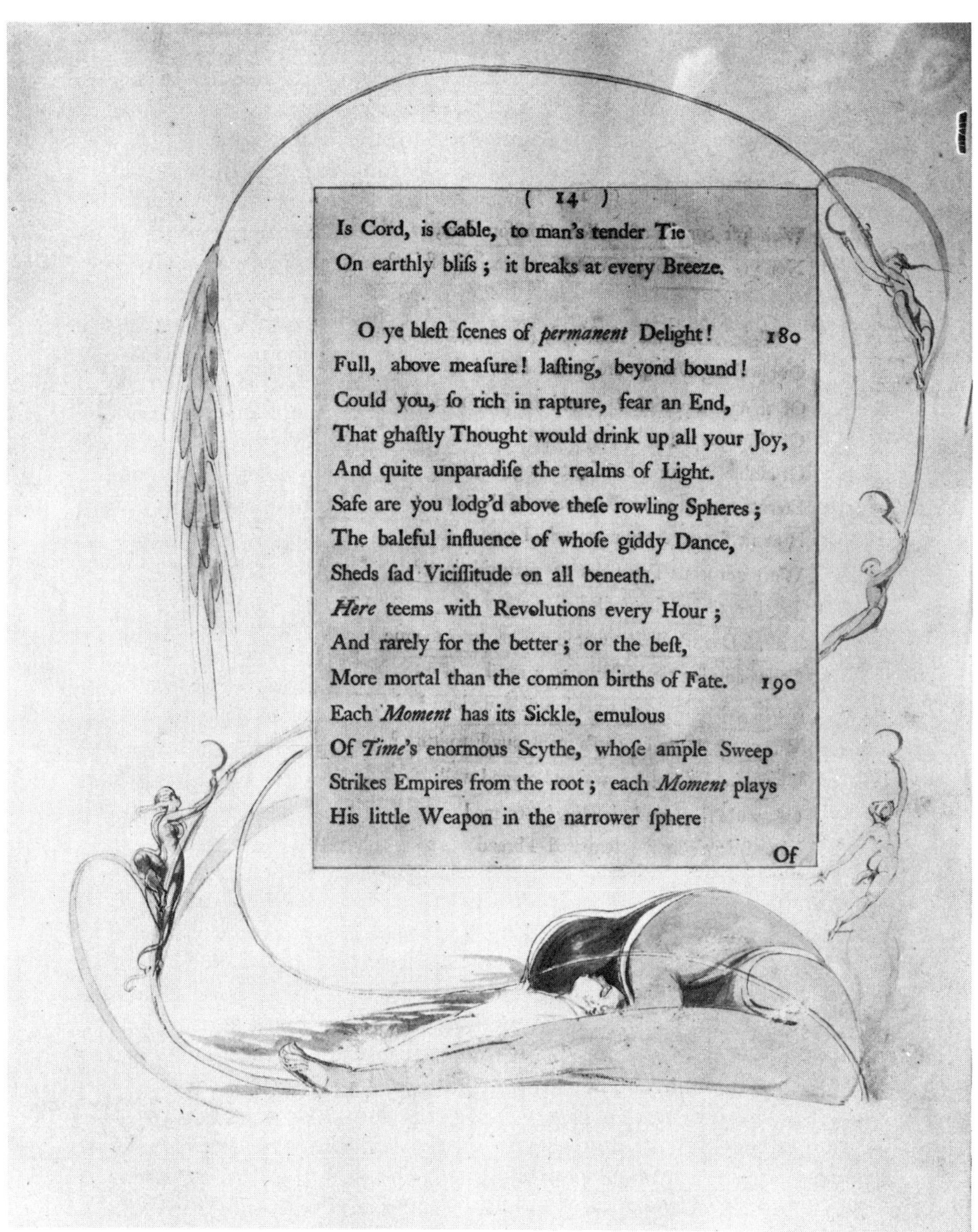

(14)

Is Cord, is Cable, to man's tender Tie
On earthly bliſs; it breaks at every Breeze.

O ye bleſt ſcenes of *permanent* Delight!
Full, above meaſure! laſting, beyond bound!
Could you, ſo rich in rapture, fear an End,
That ghaſtly Thought would drink up all your Joy,
And quite unparadiſe the realms of Light.
Safe are you lodg'd above theſe rowling Spheres;
The baleful influence of whoſe giddy Dance,
Sheds ſad Viciſſitude on all beneath.
Here teems with Revolutions every Hour;
And rarely for the better; or the beſt,
More mortal than the common births of Fate.
Each *Moment* has its Sickle, emulous
Of *Time*'s enormous Scythe, whoſe ample Sweep
Strikes Empires from the root; each *Moment* plays
His little Weapon in the narrower ſphere

Of

71 Blake, illustration to Edward Young's *Night Thoughts* 155

(46)

Like a Bird ſtruggling to get looſe, is going;
Scarce now poſſeſs'd, ſo ſuddenly 'tis gone;
And each ſwift Moment fled, is Death advanc'd
By Strides as ſwift: Eternity is All;
And whoſe Eternity? Who triumphs there?
Bathing for ever in the Font of Bliſs!
For ever baſking in the Deity!
Lorenzo! who? — Thy Conſcience ſhall reply.

O give it Leave to ſpeak; 'twill ſpeak ere long,
Thy Leave unaſkt: *Lorenzo!* hear it now,
While uſeful its Advice, its Accent mild.
By the great Edict, by divine Decree,
Truth is depoſited with Man's *laſt Hour*;
An honeſt Hour, and faithful to her Truſt.
Truth, eldeſt Daughter of the Deity;
Truth, of his Council, when he made the Worlds,
Nor leſs, when he ſhall judge the Worlds he made;
Tho' ſilent long, and ſleeping ne'er ſo ſound,
Smother'd with Errors, and oppreſt with Toys,

That

72 Blake, illustration to Edward Young's *Night Thoughts* 217

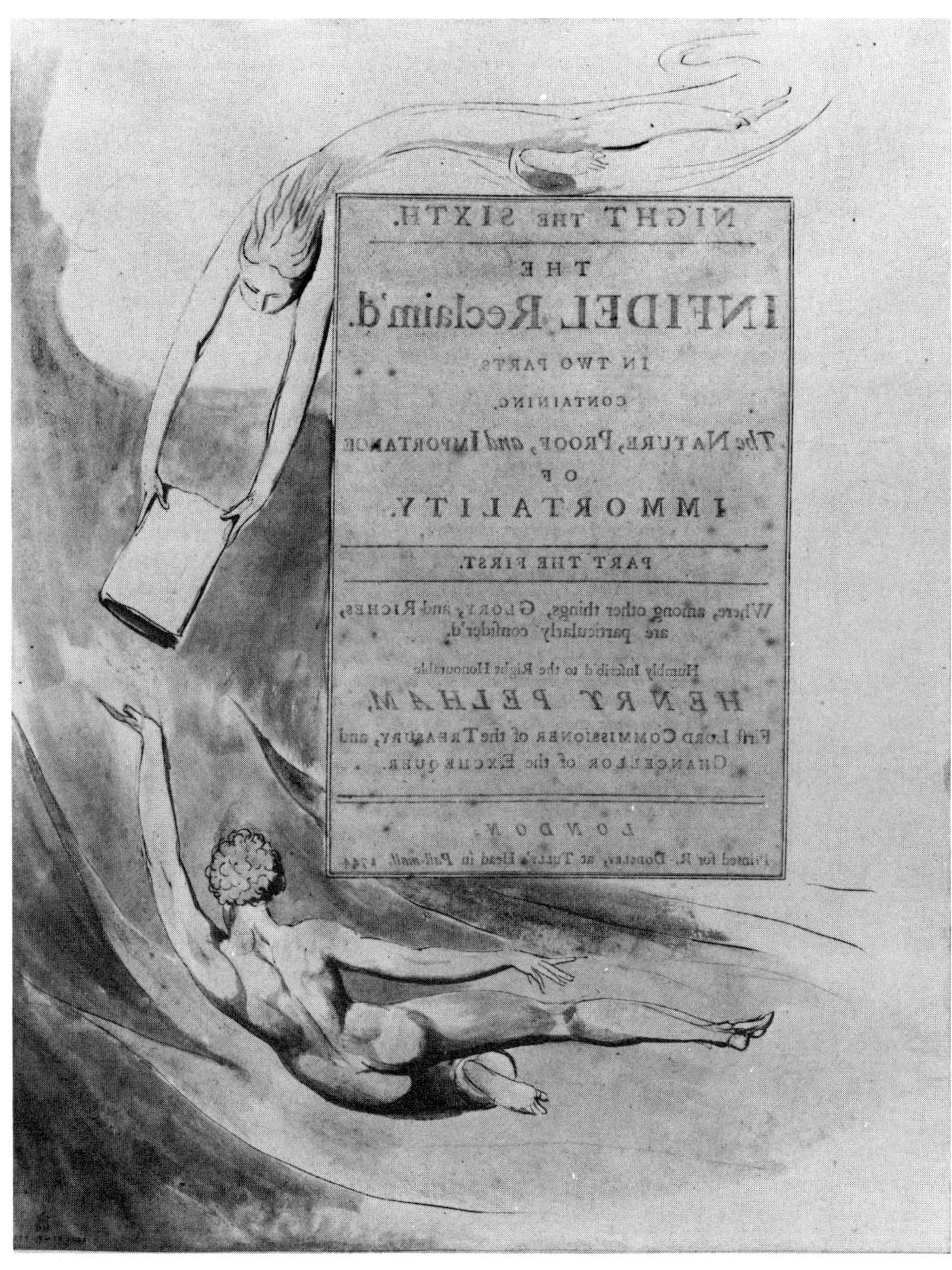

73 Blake, illustration to Thomas Gray's *The Progress of Poesy*, plate 8

74 Blake, illustration to Thomas Gray's *The Bard*, plate 12

75 Blake, *Jerusalem*, plate 46 [32]

female on the right (identified by Erdman as one of Jerusalem's daughters and by Wicksteed as Erin) because of the upward reach of her arm, which continues the thrust of the Gothic church spires underneath. This figure and the veiled one on the left act as parentheses for the three central female figures, who are commonly believed to be Jerusalem and her daughters, the veiled figure being Vala. My opinion is that the leaping form is not a *daughter* of Jerusalem but the creative energy of Jerusalem visually personified to contrast with her other aspect, the veiled Vala.

On *Jerusalem* 54, a group of soaring figures (among which the attitude I am considering is included) rises on either side of a globe labelled "This World," with the four directions named clockwise, *Reason*, *Wrath*, *Desire*, and *Pity*. The globe seems to illustrate Albion as a rocky fragment (the text: "But Albion fell down a Rocky fragment from Eternity hurld / By his own Spectre, who is the Reasoning Power in every Man ..."). The soaring forms could be energies and aspirations which have broken free or have remained free of the fall; here there is a kind of simultaneous vision of the contraries of Energy and Despair: rocky globe with the passions contained, or human forms soaring. There is also a reminder

76 Blake, illustration to Dante's *The Divine Comedy: The Whirlwind of Lovers*

77 Blake, illustration to Edward Young's *Night Thoughts*, frontispiece

that Reason and Despair are contraries, like wrath and pity, and "This World" is the rocky domain where they operate in the "memory between Man & Man."

The destructive energies of nature can also be suggested by this form, "energy rendered cruel."[3] In *Europe* 9, a singularly beautiful design, the

78 Blake, *Vala*, page 1.

79 Blake, alternative design for the title-page to Robert Blair's *The Grave: The Resurrection of the Dead*

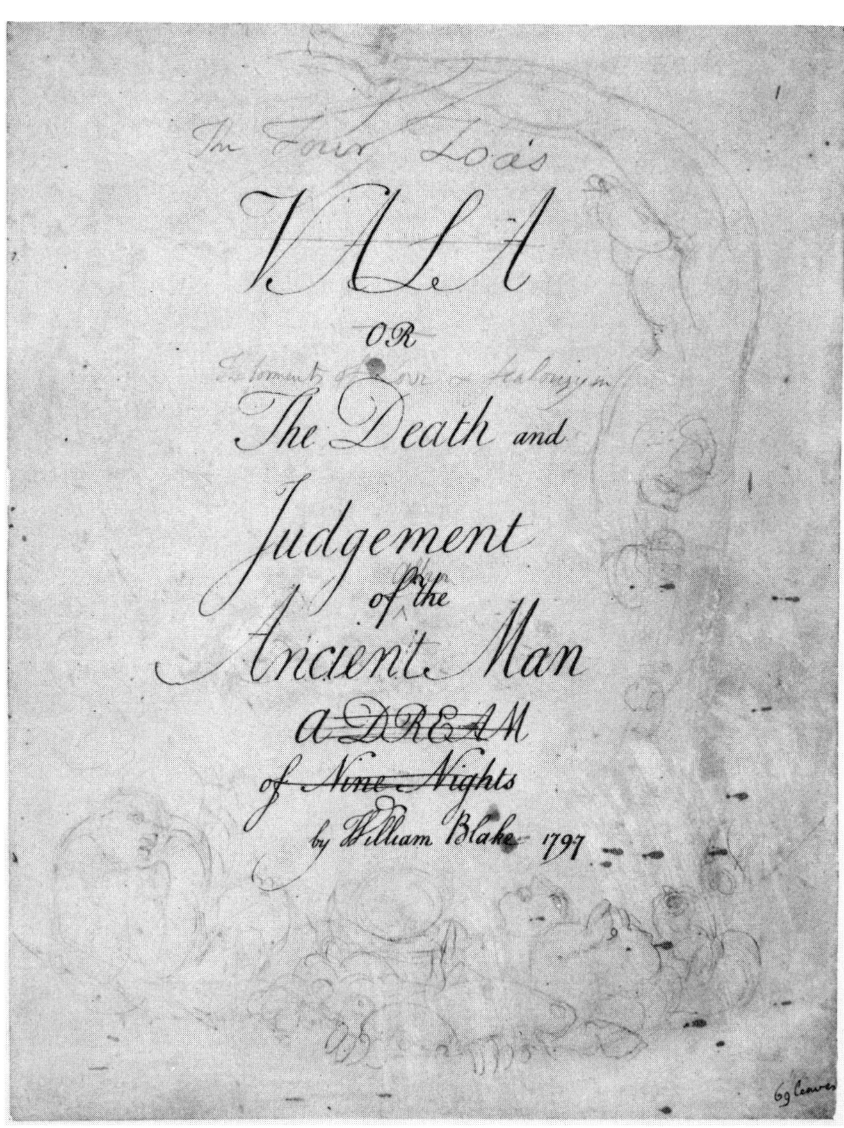

"angelic" idea (suggested by the text) still clings to the leaping forms, though they are scattering plague. Again, in Blake's design for *Paradise Lost, Satan Calling up His Legions*, we can discern this form among one of Satan's hosts. And at the end of his career Blake called upon this image to express the energy of sexual desire, in *The Whirlwind of Lovers*, one of the illustrations to Dante (specifically, the figures at "10 o'clock" in the circle; see figure 76). The contorted forms of many of the other figures in the whirlwind help to suggest that a destructive force is sweeping them along.

It is tempting to see certain upside-down attitudes and front-facing figures as variations of the leaping pose. Because mirror-imaging has an important place in Blake's art (for example, *America* 8 and 10, *Jerusalem* 76), I will be considering here the frontal or mirror images of this form, which occur in *Vala* (page 7) and the Rising Christ of *Night Thoughts* (NT 1; see figure 77). I limit mention of upside-down (that is, reversed) figures to examples which are obviously not falling but *propelling* themselves downwards, or balancing downwards, as the beautiful diving angel of *Vala* (page 1; figure 78), or the title-page to *The Grave*, or NT 38 (plate 12E engraved).

A fine illustration of Blake's use of the leaping figure and the technique of reversal to create a formal design is seen in the alternative title-page to Robert Blair's *The Grave*, a watercolour in the British Museum called *The Resurrection of the Dead* (figure 79). Here the upward-leaping and downward-propelled trumpeters provide a frame for the design and suggest the energies of resurrection. The source of this visual image, so frequent in Blake's work, appears to be a design of Henry Fuseli (figure 80). Like Blake, Fuseli was fond of formula figures, and this form was a favourite of his. Eudo Mason sees this figure as an example of Fuseli's early influence on Blake:

> Innumerable examples might be cited. But one may compare Fuseli's drawing inscribed in Greek "through the ambrosial night" and dated Rome, February 1778, where the spirit of a slain warrior, probably Sarpedon, is represented as being borne off through the air, with the sheet of Blake's *Europe* beginning with the words "Enitharmon slept ...". Nothing could be more characteristic of Fuseli, nothing more characteristic of Blake than the soaring figure with the violently foreshortened right and the long-stretched left leg – yet it is essentially one and the same figure, and Fuseli drew it before he had heard of Blake and when Blake, not yet twenty-one years old, was still in his beginnings.[4]

For Fuseli, too, the figure represented other non-corporeal energy. He was to use the form for a fairy in *The Shepherd's Dream* (figure 81) and for an angel in *Eve's Dream* (figure 82). He was also to use it for a terrific energy, Satan, in the design *Satan Flying over Chaos*. Blake tended to use the figure in much the same kinds of contexts.

The energy and movement of Fuseli's designs must have appealed very much to Blake, who at the time he met Fuseli (1787) was absorbed in the work of Swedenborg and probably of Jacob Boehme. In these writers are expressions of the ideas of flux and contraries, of creative progressions,[5] and here too are metaphors of fires of energy and mag-

80 Fuseli, from the Roman sketchbook, *Through the ambrosial night*

netic desires. As an example of Boehme's imagery, consider the following excerpt from *The Clavis, or An Explanation of Some Principal Points and Expressions*. (This is a twenty-five-page summary of Boehme's ideas, for which any modern student of this endless prose must be exceedingly grateful.)

The *Magnet*, viz. the Essential Desire of Nature, that is, the will of the Desire of Nature, compresses itself into an *Ens* or substance, to become a Plant; and in this compression of the Desire becomes feeling, that is, working; and in that working, the Power and Virtue arises, wherein the Magnetical Desire of Nature, viz. the outflown will of God works in a natural way.

In this working perceptibility, the Magnetical desiring will is elevated and made joyful, and goes forth from the working Power and Virtue; and hence comes the growing and smell of the Plant: and thus we see a representation of the Trinity of God in all growing and living things.

If there was not such a desiring perceptibility, and outgoing operation of the Trinity in the Eternal unity, the unity were but an Eternal stillness, a Nothing; and there would be no Nature, nor any Colour, Shape, or Figure; likewise there would be nothing in this world; without this threefold working, there could be no world at all. (page 6)

81 Fuseli, *The Shepherd's Dream*

Or from the *Mysterium Magnum*:

The Centre of the Eternal Nature: how the will of the Abyss brings itself into Nature and Form.

The second form or Property is the *Constringency* of the Desire; that is, a Compunction; Stirring, or *Motion*; for each Desire is attractive and constringent; and it is the Beginning of Motion, Stirring, and life ... (chapter 3, page 16)

For Boehme, another essential element in the formation of nature is fire:

82 Fuseli, *Eve's Dream*

The fourth Form of Nature is the Enkindling of the *Fire*; where the sensitive and intellective Life first arise, and the hidden God manifests himself. For without Nature he is hid to all Creatures; but in the Eternal and *Temporal Nature* he is perceived and manifest. (*Mysterium Magnum*, chapter 3, page 18)

The complex of verbal images which Blake found in Boehme, the association of desire with motion and fire, can be seen to have stimulated his visual imagination. Add to this the similar influence of Swedenborg, the wind and fire imagery of the Old Testament, and the important influence of Milton's baroque style, and we have all the necessary ingredients for the appeal of designs which transcend space, suggest swift movement (the conquest of time), and use fire as visual allegory for a divine creativity.

Contemporary science, too, could have given Blake inspiration for his soaring forms. Newton's theories of matter, energy, and attraction have been seen to reflect Neoplatonic ideas such as are present in Boehme. There has been critical controversy about Newton's Neoplatonism – or, at least, his attractiveness to Neoplatonists – ever since it was first suggested by William Law in 1782 in a letter in *Gentleman's Magazine*; however, Donald Ault has summed up the issue in this way:

The fact remains, however, that such an interpretation, correct or incorrect, is possible because the paradoxical dynamic aspect of Newton's system lends itself rather readily to such an interpretation. Such a fact illustrates, as do the interpretations of Grabo, Beach, and Priestley, that Newton's system has a strongly dynamic and unstable aspect in the constant decay and replenishment of force in the universe, which can be easily associated, by those who wish to do so, with neo-Platonic or even "mystical" cosmology. The facile similarity between energy relations in Newton's system and Boehme's is our first obvious introduction to the power of Newton's scientific system to assimilate (even if only by analogy) the whole sweep of relations contained in Blake's imaginative cosmology.[6]

Ault's book traces Blake's "metaphoric response to Newton"[7] and proves Blake to have been more involved with the scientific ideas of his time than has traditionally been believed. It is not, then, far-fetched to assume that when Blake draws figures which defy gravity, he is responding in an aesthetic way to scientific ideas, and the "sublime of energy" (in Morton Paley's term) takes visual form in images of propulsion and motion.

Three important designs in Blake's work can be illuminated by the associations that, I have been suggesting, Blake intends when he uses this form. They are the final drawing in *Vala* (page 139), the final page of *Jerusalem* (plate 100), and the Rising Christ of the frontispiece to *Night Thoughts*, volume one (*NT* 1; figure 77).

The last page of the *Vala* manuscript (139; figure 83) is dominated by

gures Energy: he Leap

the graceful form of Energy, who appears to be leaping off the curve of the earth. As John Grant notes in his discussion of this page,[8] there has been some critical disagreement regarding the sex of this figure. Damon and H.M. Margoliouth have called it female; Bentley and W.H. Stevenson regard it as male. Grant cites the rounded buttocks and long hair as signs of feminity, and in this I agree. Grant identifies her as Enitharmon, because another similar form in *Vala* (page 3) *could* be Enitharmon; I would be inclined to call her Enitharmon on the basis that she is the mirror image of the figure on the frontispiece (page 2) inscribed "Rest before Labour" and identified as Los.[9] There could, however, be another way to identify the form, and that would be to note the line of text

83 Blake, *Vala*, last page

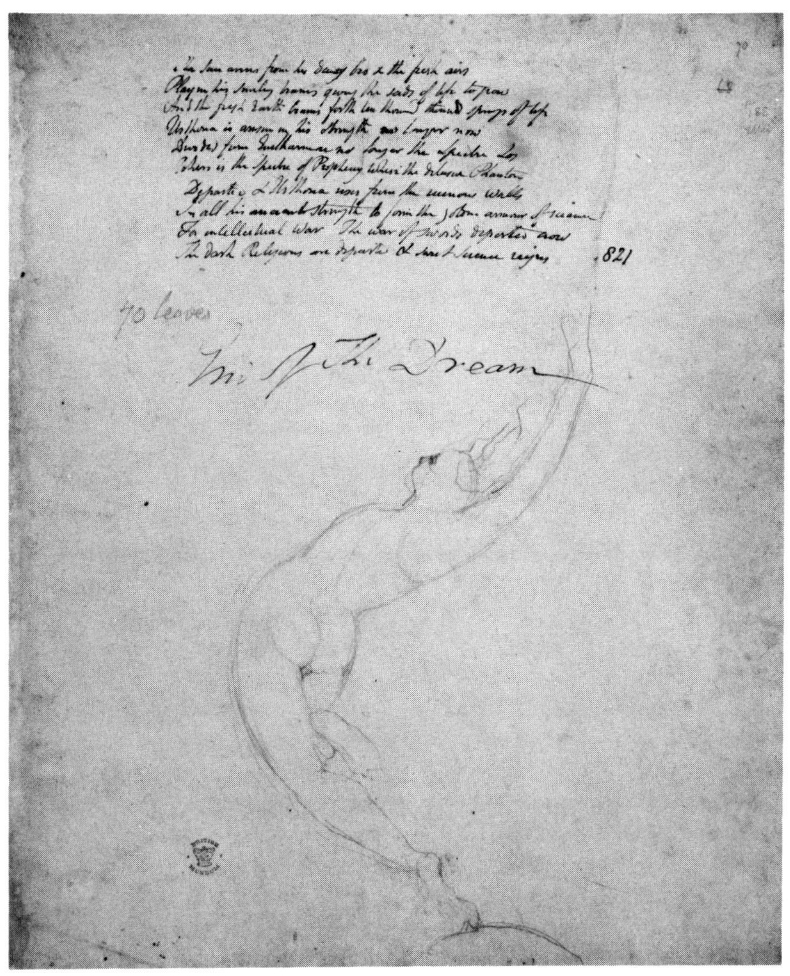

which reads: "And the fresh Earth beams forth ten thousand thousand springs of life" (page 139). The design could well represent these essential energetic forces of nature; it could also be a kind of visual pun on "springs" of life. The "beaming forth" of the earth identifies it metaphorically with the sun, so that the curved line in the design from which the figure springs could also stand for the sun. And the poetry here connects the final plate with page 2 and its springing man with rays of light behind him.[10] Of course, none of this prevents us calling the figure Enitharmon; it merely complicates the associations and deepens the symbolic significance of the design.

Grant expresses intimations of connections between *Vala* page 2, and *Jerusalem* 100, and I would suggest that the connection includes *Vala*, page 139. In *Jerusalem* 100 we see the familiar Energy figure leaping from the earth, carrying the sun on his back (figure 84). The musculature of the nude suggests that he is male, and in the centre is another male nude, with hammer and compasses, standing in the "Apollo" attitude that Blake has used so often for regenerated states (for example, Milton, Satan in his original glory, Adam). The central figure is generally identified as Los, and the female figure with shuttle and stars, Enitharmon. However, the figure carrying the sun is variously identified. Erdman and Paley call him the Spectre of Urthona, while Damon refers

84 Blake, *Jerusalem*, plate 100

to Los's Spectre.[11] These are not exactly the same, but Blake has been most confusing, and the critics have not helped. Blake seems to have started out in *Jerusalem* using the terms interchangeably, as in plate 10, where in line 18 the term is "his Spectre" (that is, Los's), in line 19 "the Spectre," and in line 32, "Spectre of Urthona." Very soon Blake refers only to *the* Spectre, who identifies himself to Albion with the words, "I am your Rational Power" (*J* 29: 5). The Spectre of Urthona also represents the despair that results from too much rationality, and there is no reason to suppose that the Spectre of Albion is any different from the one who speaks to Los in plate 10. Rationality and despair, then, are attributes of the Spectre, and as I have indicated previously, their visual shapes are the rounded, huddled attitudes so common in the *Book of Urizen*.

The question then arises: why would we have a Spectre depicted on plate 100 in a visual form which Blake has consistently used for energy, for the *opposite* of spectral shapes? I do not think that Blake intends us to see that figure as a Spectre at all but rather as the most creative form of natural energy, which is Urizen, Prince of Light (Reason, the bound or outward circumference of Energy). Or, to put it another way, we can call the figure in the centre Urthona-Los, framed by his Emanation Enitharmon and his Eternal Counterpart Urizen. The connections between them may be implied in the exchange of symbols – Urizen is carrying the sun for Los (plate 94 and the frontispiece), and Los has his hammer and compass-like tongs.

The careful reader may now wish to reconsider the identity of the pencil sketch on *Vala*, page 2. The inscription "Rest Before Labour" seems to be in the spirit of the last lines of *Jerusalem*, and the figure is the mirror image of the sun-carrier in *J* 100, as has been noted. Instead of identifying this figure as Los, perhaps one should think of him as the Urizen of *Vala*, Night II, described as rising "from the Banquet Feast like a star thro' the evening sky." Certainly in *Vala*, Los and Urizen share the sun symbol (compare the designs for Night IV: 47 and Night VI: 74 and 75), and the text of Night VI speaks of Urizen thus:

> Still he with his globe of fire immense in his venturous hand
> Bore on thro the Affrighted vales ascending & descending
> (*FZ* VI: 74; E 351).

The mirror image of the leaping Energy form (which has been my starting point) is also used to powerful effect by Blake for the Rising Christ of the *Night Thoughts* frontispiece (*NT* 1; see also page 114 of *Vala*). This image brings together all the associations of movement, aspiration, creativity, and sunlight we have been discussing. It is a design which to my mind echoes visually the language of Henry Fuseli, defining terms he will use in his art lectures at the Royal Academy in 1801:

By *grace* I mean that artless balance of motion and repose spring from character, founded on propriety, which neither falls short of the demands nor overleaps the modesty of nature.[12]

When the editors of *William Blake's Designs for Edward Young's Night Thoughts* discuss the title-pages for the watercolour designs, they note that Blake's placing of this design as the fourth title-page of the engraved edition indicates the triumph of Christianity as a foil for Young's melancholy. Yet it also suggests the *energy* which is a foil for the languid poet. This Christ reminds us of the Christ of Blake's *Everlasting Gospel*, not passive and suffering but proud and active, "bursting forth his furious ire" and becoming a "Chariot of fire" (E 523). The editors of the *Night Thoughts* designs write of this design as "the conscious sunburst of a merciful illumination" (volume 1, page 37), referring to the importance of the light radiating from the figure. A last note by John Grant is particularly interesting, pointing out variations of this frontal attitude as well as its relation to designs I have been discussing:

Even viewers who have adjusted to the far greater distortions of twentieth century art are occasionally displeased with the energetic, long, manneristic swing of the left leg of Christ, twisted into an anatomically improbable relation to the drawn-up right knee and shin. It is evident that Blake himself was happy with this formula, since he has variations of it in NT 11, the Traveller, NT 14, the Cavorter, NT 229, the rising spirit, etc. The formula is repeated exactly in NT 38 (13E) with right and left legs interchanged, in the great picture of the diving trumpeter awakening the skeleton. The motif was used again in the title page for *Vala* or *The Four Zoas*, Blake's own Dream of Nine Nights.[13]

The image of Christ is central to Blake's interpretation of Young's *Night Thoughts* and provides a Blakean comment on Young regarding the importance of Christ as Imagination. For him to have chosen this leaping attitude for one of Christ's depictions means that Blake intended to incorporate in the Christ figure the associations of a humanized nature, a moment incarnated, a desire realized, and energy concentrated.

From surveying the importance of the leaping form in Blake's visual vocabulary, we may realize that there is significance also in the occasions when he chooses *not* to use it. We do not, for instance, see Orc or Satan, those supreme symbols of Blakean energy, depicted in this way. This supports my suggestion that Blake often distinguishes elemental forces from his cast of "characters" and that by showing us a *leaping* Christ he suggests the incarnate unity of body and spirit in his own visual shorthand.

And what of figures in Blake's designs that are gravity-free, who soar but do not leap? They abound in his work, but are particularly evident in the surviving designs for *The Last Judgment*.[14] In his written descriptions of this work Blake makes distinctions regarding kinds of movement. The Just "rise thro the Air ... the Blessed ... arise upon the Air rejoicing" (E 553). Satan is described as "falling headlong," while Death is "dragged down" by a demon. Another figure is "precipitating himself" (E 556). However, four angels "*descend* headlong with four trumpets to awake the Dead" (E 558; emphasis added). In the Pollock House design, these angels are depicted in the same upside-down leaping form we have seen so often before (see figures 78 and 105). I suggest therefore that figures who rise and fall are governed by powers other than their own, while figures who *descend* are pictured in that attitude to suggest autonomous energy. The soaring straight-legged figures are drawn upwards as if attracted by a magnetic force; the leaping figures themselves contain that force.

We may see these contrasting motions again in a comparison of Blake's lovely design *The River of Life* (figure 85) and the dynamic title-page to *The Marriage of Heaven and Hell* (figure 86). In the *MHH* title-page, embracing couples, the most obvious pair face-to-face in horizontal atti-

85 Blake, *The River of Life*

86 Blake, *The Marriage of Heaven and Hell*, title-page

tudes, rise up on flames and smoke towards the line of earth and trees, where other couples are walking or reclining. There are no leaping figures that I can discern in the picture. The energy – that is, the movement – of the design comes from the lines of flame and tree and from the flaming lines of the word "marriage." The soaring forms are borne upwards on the flames; and like most of the figures in Blake's later design for Dante's *The Whirlwind of Lovers* (see figure 76) they are carried along by a force they do not control, a force of energy and desire, here symbolized by flame and air. (Blake managed to include *all* the elements, earth, air, fire, and water, in the Dante design.) The *MHH* design suggests to me that a lid is placed on all this energy by the surface line of earth, which is conveniently labelled HEAVEN. This idea is borne out, of course, by the work, which explores and reverses the meaning of such labels as Heaven and Hell and gives the Devil all the best lines, while the angels are prosaic and earthbound. When the voice of the Devil (plate 5) comments upon restrained desire becoming passive and therefore the "shadow" of desire, we may think of the strolling and reclining figures on the earth-line of the title-page.[15]

By way of contrast, Blake's watercolour called *The River of Life* depicts the source of energy in the human figures themselves, by using the leaping pose. Here an Energy figure descends from the sun, whose rays are humanized. Two childish figures and one adult are presumably swimming towards the sun figure; their attitudes almost mirror his. This is the only occasion I have found of the "leap" in water rather than in air. Three other figures in the picture are walking on the water. They are the musicians on either side of the page and the bending woman whose reaching arm mirrors the sun figure's gesture, providing yet another "frame" for the action. The three swimmers are swimming upstream towards the sun figure. Joseph Wicksteed identifies these as "Christ leading two children through the stream of time towards the divine sun while to the right the Bride (the New Jerusalem) swoops down to sever the thread of remembrance."[16] Since there is an interesting mix of the Hebraic and the Greek in this picture (if we are to take seriously the inscription's reference to Revelation 22 and also to consider the architecture of the buildings), I think it more likely that the stooping figure is the Fate Atropos.[17] The paradox of the design is that the Hebraic River of Life is the Greek river of forgetfulness. These children are being born into spiritual life, their mortal existence and memory severed. The contemplation of these two designs reminds us again of the close association of energy and desire in Blake's thought.

Behind the sun figure in the River of Life, the rays of the sun are humanized as single angels and embracing couples, the same embracing couples as on the *MHH* title-page. The source of desire is the River of Life, Blake seems to be telling us, and the power of desire is manifested by those who soar in flames.

SIX

Figures of Energy: The Dance

Although the dance is perhaps the most familiar and expressive means by which any of us perceives a visual language, it does not seem to have captured Blake's imagination in a positive way. The emblematic attitude which he used for a dancing figure is, of course, the stunning *Albion Rose*; yet the dance that Albion is performing, as we know from the inscription on the engraving, is the "Dance of Eternal Death" (figure 49). There are a few cheerful dancing groups in Blake's designs, but in his poetry we find that dancing is most often sadistic or masochistic, and symbolic of the depths of the fallen world. Why this should be so is hard to fathom; nevertheless, unlike Blake's leaping or soaring figures, his dancing figures are usually gravity-bound,[1] tied to the earth in spite of the airy quality of their movements. Blake must have perceived live dancers in this way. Certainly there is an ambivalence regarding the dance in his work which we can find as early as the song of "The Chimney Sweeper" of *Experience*, who says:

> And because I am happy, & dance & sing,
> They think they have done me no injury.

Dancing is only the appearance of happiness.

And yet Blake's designs have inspired dance performances in this century, ever since Sir Geoffrey Keynes, Ralph Vaughan-Williams, and Gwen Raverat first produced *Job, A Masque for Dancing* in 1927. Because the *Job* designs are so full of narrative gesture, it is not surprising that their balletic possibilities have been so brilliantly realized.

Still, it is the movement of modern dance, not traditional leaps and pirouettes, which twentieth-century choreographers perceive in Blake's designs. The dances that Blake himself could have been familiar with are those of folk-dancing, of pantomime, and of the French-influenced ballet on the eighteenth-century English stage. There was also available to him the artistic depiction of Greek maenads or warriors in the drawings and engravings of acquaintances who had been to Italy, or the designs in D'Hancarville's volume of Sir William Hamilton's collection of Greek

87 Faun, from a personal album of George Cumberland

vases (1766). In George Cumberland's personal album of outlines which categorized types of action and gesture, "enthusiastic action" is always a dancing figure of the kind Blake used for *The Goblin* in his illustrations for Milton's *L'Allegro* and *Il Penseroso* (figures 87 and 88).

Indeed, "enthusiasm" is a concept directly related to Blake's ideas of energy, with its associations in the eighteenth century of prophetic possession. However, Blake's attitude to enthusiastic dancing was closely

88 Blake, illustration to Milton's *L'Allegro* and *Il Penseroso: The Goblin*

linked to his idea of aesthetic decorum. When he wrote in his *Descriptive Catalogue* of the visual equivalents for the Beautiful, Strong, and Ugly men, he was aware that the prevailing model for the Ugly Man was the dancing faun:

> It has been said to the Artist, take the Apollo for the model of your beautiful Man and the Hercules for your strong Man, and the Dancing Fawn for your Ugly Man.[2]

Though Blake does not describe his own Ugly Man as dancing (in his account of his painting *The Ancient Britons* in the *Descriptive Catalogue*), he does say he is "approaching to the beast in features and form, his forehead small, without frontals; his jaws large; his nose high on the ridge, and narrow ... everything tending to what is truly Ugly; the incapability of intellect" (E 544–5). The antique sculptures or other representations of the dancing faun which were familiar to eighteenth-century artists depict half-human male figures with tails and horns, whose erect penises imply that possession of intellect is not one of their concerns. (Cumberland's drawing of "enthusiastic action" is a copy of one of these; see figure 87.)

What then are we to make of *Albion Rose*, obviously dancing yet obvi-

89 Blake, *Oberon, Titania and Puck with Fairies Dancing*

ously beautiful, even though his dance, according to the caption, is a dance of death? Our answer to this question must come after a survey of Blake's major dancing figures and groups, and relevant poetic passages. To begin, however, the dance world of late eighteenth-century London can provide us with a context for Blake's dancing figures.

England has always been rich in folk-dance tradition, the sword dance, the Morris dance and the country dance having flourished there as they did in other countries. The Morris and sword dances were danced by men only and were ritual dances performed usually at specific seasons, the sword dance between Christmas and New Year to symbolize the death of the old year, the Morris dance in the spring. The country dance was danced by men and women in couples and became a social dance: Cecil Sharp writes that it was derived from the May Day dance and became a favourite alternative to the more formal galliards and pavanes at the court of Elizabeth.[3] It is the country dance that we see Blake illustrating when he draws fairies dancing in a ring, as in the watercolour *Oberon, Titania and Puck with Fairies Dancing* (1785; see figure 89). Running and skipping movements are the bases of these dances; the English country dance was what people enjoyed at weddings and at fairs. In the early eighteenth century it was exported to France, where it became known as the *contredanse*. It then came back to England as fashionable. Cecil Sharp writes:

> In England even at the end of the 18th century the Ball sometimes opened with a Promenade round the room in couples to a marching tune ... Then Minuets were danced – at Bath Beau Nash always led the first. Thereafter none but Country Dances were danced.[4]

As well as the popular rooms at Bath, there opened in London in the second half of the eighteenth century a number of elegant assembly rooms to cater to the demand for indoor social dancing: Carlisle House in Soho Square (1763), Almack's in King Street, St James (1765), the Pantheon in Oxford Street (1772), and the Argyll Rooms in Regent Street.[5] Blake, not a member of fashionable society, nevertheless knew enough of it to enjoy satirizing its traditional dancing habits when he illustrated Thomas Gray's poetry. We find in *A Long Story* the description of "my grave Lord-Keeper" leading "The Brawls" – that is, the *branle* or country-dance promenade that had opened a ball since Elizabethan times:

> Full oft within the spacious walls,
> When he had fifty winters o'er him,
> My grave Lord-Keeper led the Brawls:
> The Seals and Maces danc'd before him.[6]

Blake's illustration for this shows a dandified Elizabethan gentleman and

90 Blake, illustration to Thomas Gray's *A Long Story*

a personified dancing Mace and Elizabethan Seal (see figure 90), almost like a Rowlandson cartoon.

Classical dancing, as distinguished from folk or country dancing, began in the French court and came to England through French performers and the productions of the dancing-master Jean-Georges Noverre (1727–1809). In London, in 1783, the English translation of one of the cornerstones of dance literature was published, Noverre's *Letters on Dancing* (1760). Noverre was called "the Shakespeare of the Dance" by David Garrick, who invited him and his *corps de ballet* to London from Paris in 1754 to perform at Drury Lane.[7] Since the opening coincided with the outbreak of the Seven Years' War, a riot ensued in the theatre because a French company was performing, and all the stage effects were destroyed. All this happened before Blake was born, but Noverre came twice more to London almost thirty years later, when he was *maître de ballet* to the Kings Theatre (now the Haymarket) for the seasons 1780–1 and 1781–2 and again at the outbreak of the French Revolution, when his company included the famous dancers Vestris and Mlle Guimard. Cyril Beaumont's account gives us some idea of the dance scene in the late 1780s:

> There on January 29th 1788, he produced his *L'Amour et Psyche* with a company that included Vestris, Didelot and Coulon. On March 13th he staged *Euthyme et Eucharis* for Vestris' benefit, and on April 17th he gave *Adele et Ponthieu*. The year following, on June 17th, the "Kings" was burned to the ground. It was rebuilt in 1790 and reopened on March 26, 1791 with Noverre as director, Vestris as *maitre de ballet*, Hayden as composer, and Federici as conductor.[8]

We do not know if Blake ever attended performances of ballet, but Fuseli was enthusiastic about it, and it is likely that the name of Noverre was known to Blake at least by 1790, when Noverre was famous (or infamous) for his *Letters* and vigorous reform of dancing style. Like other writers on the arts in the eighteenth century, Noverre constantly used the metaphor of painting to make his points, in this case about the dance:

> A ballet is a picture, or rather a series of pictures connected one with the other by the plot which provides the theme of the ballet; the image is, as it were, the canvas on which the composer expresses his ideas; the choice of the music, scenery and costumes are his colours; the composer is the painter. (Letter 1, Beaumont, trans., *Letters*, page 9)

Noverre also saw painting and dancing as visual languages:

> Painting and dancing have this advantage over the other arts, that they are of every country, of all nations; that their language is universally understood, and

91 Gainsborough, *Giovanna Baccelli*

that they achieve the same impression everywhere. (Letter IV, page 28)

He urged composers of dance to study and copy painters, and advised the study of anatomy and drawing:

A composer who desires to rise above his fellows should study painters and copy them in their different methods of design and execution. Both arts have the same object in view whether it be for the achieving of likeness, the admixture of colours, the play of light and shade, or the grouping and draping of figures, posing them in graceful attitudes and giving them character, life and expression; but now, how can a *maître de ballet* hope to succeed if he does not possess the abilities and qualities which go to the making of an eminent painter? (Letter V, page 29)

All of this Blake might be expected to approve.

Of special interest in this ballet background, against which Blake's "dancing" designs emerge, is the tradition of the attitudes or poses in which dancers were pictured. Many of the best-known dancers of the day were painted or drawn in dance positions, as we see in Thomas Gainsborough's painting of Giovanna Baccelli (figure 91), exhibited in 1782. Frequently, famous dancers were pictured in the step known as *balancé* (see figures 92 and 93). We recognize this as the position of *Albion Rose*, which we now see even more reason for calling *The Dance of Albion*. I believe we can now add ballet illustration to the sources usually attributed to this design – the Vitruvian figure, the faun from Herculaneum, and the outstretched arms of crucifixion. Yet Albion's dance, which is our touchstone in this chapter, deserves further exploration. The activity of dancing in Blake's poetry is seldom positive, and to his poetry we shall now turn.

It is not an exaggeration to say that dancing in Blake's mature poetry is always ambivalent and often overwhelmingly orgiastic and destructive.[9] The most memorable instance of this is the dance of Los at the end of Night IV in *The Four Zoas*. It marks the creation of the fallen body:

Spasms siezd his muscular fibres writhing to & fro his pallid lips
Unwilling movd as Urizen howld his loins wavd like the sea ...
The bones of Urizen hurtle on the wind the bones of Los
Twinge & his iron sinews bend like lead & fold
Into unusual forms dancing & howling stamping the Abyss
(FZ IV: 55; E 338).

This dance is continued at the beginning of Night V: "Infected Mad be dancd on his mountains high & dark as heaven" (E 338). This is a dance of disease – probably, in Blake's mind, St Vitus's Dance, the religious dancing mania of the Middle Ages in Europe. Even the weather is expressed in the metaphor of a dance of death, the "chain" being a dance figure:

92 *Mlle Hiligsberg*

Grim frost beneath & terrible snow linkd in a marriage chain
Began a dismal dance. (*FZ* v: 58; E339)

The intellectual background for this attitude to dance was close at hand. Its primary source for Blake was probably the Bible. There is much dancing in the Old Testament, and Blake may have regarded it as homage to tyranny. In 1799 he had illustrated *Moses Indignant at the Golden Calf* (Exod. 32:19), which shows in the background naked idolatrous dancers worshipping the golden calf. Jephtha's daughter, soon to be sacrificed, is shown dancing out to meet her father in Blake's painting of that subject. In the Old Testament, we read that David danced before the Lord "with all his might," much to the disgust of Saul's daughter (2 Sam. 6). Worship through dance was instructed in the Psalms of David: "Let them praise his name in the dance: let them sing praises unto him with the timbrel and bays" (Ps. 149); "Praise him with timbrel and dance" (Ps. 150).

Blake appears to adopt these images in the Dionysiac dance of Gwendolyn in *Jerusalem* 58:

93 Lancret, *Madame Camargo*

94 Blake, illustration to G.A. Burger's *Lenore*, frontispiece

O! how I dreamt of things impoſsible,
Of Death affecting Forms least like himself;
I've seen, or dreamt I saw the Tyrant dreſs,
Lay by his Horrors, and put on his Smiles;

Treacherous he came an unexpected Guest,
Nay, though invited by the loudest Calls
Of blind Imprudence, unexpected still;
And then, he dropt his Mask.

Alter'd from Young.

Naked & drunk with blood Gwendolen dancing to the timbrel
Of War ... (*J* 58: 2–3)

Altogether, the image of dance in *Jerusalem* is associated with horror and war. The sons and daughters of Albion dance madly and bloodily all through chapter 3: weaving and dancing in bloody garments become familiar Blakean metaphors for the worst aspects of the material world.[10] The illustration on plate 69 depicts a dance of ritual torture. In *Milton*, too, Blake wrote of the creation of the fallen body to the accompaniment of "the dance of tears & pain" (*M* 5, E 98), and in an extraordinary passage which combines music with an evocation of the human digestive system, Blake includes a reference to the dance of death (*M* 24, E 121). In passages such as these, we sense something medieval in Blake, a verbal echo of the many graphic representations of the dance of death: death coming to all, high-born or low, present at the feast. For Blake, he dances before dead England's hearse, the personified cry and curse of the harlot and gambler.

Blake's own graphic versions of the dance of death may be found in his frontispiece for J.T. Stanley's version of G.A. Burger's *Lenore* (London 1796; figure 94) and in *Night Thoughts* 205 (figure 95). The former picture is grotesque and the latter lyrical in tone, yet each suggests that medieval awareness: *timor mortis conturbat me*. The carefree, unaware dancers of the *Night Thoughts* design strike a pose not unlike *Albion Rose*, and heedlees Vanity dances on the very edge of the grave in *Night Thoughts* 253 (figure 96). John Grant considers that all these pictures throw light on the meaning of Blake's *Mirth and Her Companions*, an illustration for the series of designs to Milton's *L'Allegro* and *Il Penseroso* which is of interest to us too in the context of dance.[11]

In John Milton, Blake found an author whose metaphors stimulated his imagination in many ways, resulting in several unusual examples of dancing designs. Blake plays with Milton's lines, realizing them in visual images which take the ideas in new directions.[12] The works which are especially relevant here are two designs of the twelve for Milton's *L'Allegro* and *Il Penseroso* (1817) and some of the set of illustrations to *Comus* (1801 and 1805).

The general consensus regarding the *L'Allegro* and *Il Penseroso* designs is that they are Blake's commentary on the poetic development of Milton from pastoral poet to prophet.[13] Some of the designs may also be paired (for example, *Mirth* and *Melancholy*) in the way that the two halves of Milton's poem may be paired and contrasted. Critics have seen a kind of Innocence-Experience pattern in them, though this approach does not get us very far and, as E.J. Rose has noted, is "only ancillary to the poetical concerns" of the works. These are among the most crowded of Blake's designs and not, I think, among his most attractive. Yet they provide a fascinating exercise in "reading" Blake's pictures. The pictures I will examine here are *Mirth* and *The Goblin*.

95 Blake, illustration to Edward Young's *Night Thoughts* 205

(50)

A pamper'd Spendthrift; whoſe fantaſtic Air,
Well faſhion'd Figure, and cockaded Brow,
He took in change, and underneath the Pride
Of coſtly Linnen, tuck'd his filthy Shroud.
His crooked Bow he ſtraightned to a Cane;
And hid his deadly Shafts in *Myra*'s Eye.
The dreadful Maſquerader thus equipt,
Out-Sallies on Adventures. Aſk you where?
Where is He not? For his peculiar haunts,
Let *this* ſuffice; ſure as Night follows Day,
Death treads in *Pleaſure*'s footſteps round the World,
When *Pleaſure* treads the Paths, which *Reaſon* ſhuns.
When, againſt *Reaſon*, *Riot* ſhuts the door,
And *Gayety* ſupplies the Place of *Senſe*,
Then foremoſt at the Banquet, and the Ball,
Death leads the Dance, or ſtamps the deadly Die;
Nor ever fails the Midnight Bowl to crown.
Gayly carouſing to his gay Compeers,
Inly he laughs, to ſee them laugh at him,
As Abſent far; and when the Revel burns,

When

96 Blake, illustration to Edward Young's *Night Thoughts* 253

(32)

Expects an Empire? He forgets his Chain,
And thron'd in Thought, his abſent ſcepter waves.
 And what a Scepter waits us? What a Throne?
Her own immenſe Apointments to compute,
Or comprehend her high Prerogatives,
In this her dark Minority, how toils,
How vainly pants, the human ſoul Divine?
Too great the bounty ſeems for Earthly joy;
What heart but trembles at ſo ſtrange a Bliſs?
 In ſpite of all the Truths the Muſe has ſung,
Truths touching! marvellous! and full of Heaven!
Ne'er to be priz'd enough! enough revolv'd!
Are there, who wrap the World ſo cloſe about them,
They ſee no farther than the Clouds; and dance
On heedleſs Vanity's phantaſtic Toe,
Till ſtumbling at a Straw, in their career,
Headlong they plunge, where end both dance, and ſong?
Are there *Lorenzo!* Is it poſſible?
Are there on Earth (let me not call them Men)
Who lodge a ſoul Immortal in their breaſts;

Un-

At the beginning of *L'Allegro*, Milton summons "heart-easing Mirth":

Haste thee nymph, and bring with thee
Jest and youthful Jollity,
Quips and Cranks, and Wanton Wiles,
Nods, and Becks, and Wreathed Smiles ...

97 Blake, *Mirth and Her Companions*

igures
Energy:
he Dance

Sport that wrinkled Care derides
And Laughter holding both his sides.
Come, and trip it as ye go
On the light fantastick toe ...

Blake's first design for this series is *Mirth and Her Companions* (figure 97). The design also exists in two engraved states. John Grant asks two pertinent questions of these designs: What is the matter with Mirth? and What are all those golden builders up to anyway? Are there destroyers among them? After carefully examining every character in the picture and its analogues in other designs, Grant (who is not easy to follow) concludes that Mirth is in peculiar and ambivalent company. I agree with him. Grant did not emphasize the activity of dancing *per se* in these pictures but examined the rather grotesque physical attributes of Mirth's companions (cat whiskers, batwings and asses' ears). He recalls Blake's own statement about Mirth and reflects upon her "middle position":

> Fun I love but too much Fun is of all things the most loathsom Mirth is better than Fun & Happiness is better than Mirth ... (Letter to Trusler, 23 August 1799; E 676)

98 Blake, *Eve Tempted by the Serpent*

Grant concludes that there are contrasting moral groups surrounding Mirth in Blake's designs and that they are "all in jeopardy."

Blake has here, I suggest, given us a female version of *Albion Rose*. An energetic and powerful central dancing figure is accompanied by ambiguous symbolic images – in Albion's case the batwinged moth and in Mirth's case her grotesque companions. While Albion's alternate form can be seen as Satan in *Job* 6, Mirth's may be Eve in *Eve Tempted by the Serpent* (see figure 98). Thus the "Goodes fair and free" of Milton's *L'Allegro* could be spurned as one of "the blood of folly without father bred" of *Il Penseroso*. Blake always makes us aware of the simultaneous existence of the shadow realm. There is then more to his illustration of Mirth than the existence of her contrary within the poem, Melancholy. Mirth is a delightful but precarious companion. Surely Blake was only being half ironic when, to the second engraved state of the design, he added an inscription: "Solomon says Vanity of Vanities all is Vanity & what can be Foolisher than this" (E 686).

The Goblin (*L'Allegro*, plate 5; figure 88) is another illustration in this series which has perplexed critics. It belongs in the Innocence half of Milton's poem, yet as Martin Butlin has remarked of it, "Something seems to have gone very wrong with mirthful Innocence."[14] E.J. Rose suggests that the design represents Shakespearean dream-poetry in the education of Milton; Grant describes but does not attempt to interpret it; Stephen Behrendt most plausibly suggests that the design depicts the "perverse spirits at large in the World of Experience."[15]

Blake tells us that he has literally illustrated Milton's lines. He inscribes the words thus:

> Then to the Spicy Nut brown Ale
> With Stories told of many a Treat
> How Fairy Mab the junkets eat
> She was punchd & pulld she said
> And he by Friars Lantern led
> Tells how the drudging Goblin sweat
> To earn his Cream Bowl duly set
> When in one Night e'er glimpse of Morn
> His shadowy Flail had threshd the Corn
> That ten day labourers could not end
> Then crop-full out of door he flings
> E'er the first Cock his Matin rings

The Goblin crop full flings out of doors from his Laborious task dropping his Flail & Cream bowl. Yawning & stretching vanishes into the Sky in which is seen Queen Mab Eating the Junkets. The Sports of the Fairies are seen thro the Cottage where "She" lays in Bed "pinched & pulld" by Fairies as they dance on the Bed the Cieling & the Floor & a Ghost pulls the Bed Clothes at her Feet. "He" is seen following the Friars Lantern towards the Convent (Blake's inscription, E 683)

Blake's Goblin yawns and stretches in dance-like posture reminiscent of the dancing faun. He is transparent, for he is vanishing into the sky. He makes the design, as Butlin notes, an image of horror. This is quite the opposite of the effect of the incident in Milton's poem, where the ghost stories are told in a group, with the comforting accompaniment of "Spicy Nut brown Ale." If these designs are Blake's analysis of the progress of Milton's imagination, then this design is as important as *Mirth* or *Melancholy* or *The Great Sun* and underlines the importance of strangeness and terror in the development of a poet. The energy of the Goblin's dance suggests a connection between him and the maypole dancers in the previous design, *A Sunshine Holiday*: in effect the Goblin culminates the dancing of the *L'Allegro* which began with *Mirth*. There are no more dancing figures in these designs, for the poet of *The Youthful Poet's Dream* (plate 6) must assimilate these energies to the "more bright Sun of Imagination under the auspices of Shakespeare & Johnson ... (E 684).

With these words Blake may be reminding us of the existence of Milton's *Comus*. The tutelage of Jonson stimulated Milton's creation of a masque, and Milton's poem in turn inspired two sets of designs from Blake. Dancing was a main feature of the English masque, and though Milton's *Comus* was as much intended as a lesson in morality as a stage spectacle, there were dances in it. Marcia Pointon notes that *Comus* was one of the most popular entertainments of the eighteenth century, an adapted stage version having gone through over thirty printings.[16] Many eighteenth-century artists produced illustrations of *Comus*, all influenced by the stage productions.[17] Blake's designs for *Comus* are not theatrical and do indeed have the meditative, "inward" quality that Angus Fletcher has suggested of them,[18] but do they convey a criticism of Milton which has been lost on some commentators, as Stephen Behrendt suggests?

In his persuasive but, I think, wrongly focused article on Blake's *Comus* designs, Behrendt argues that Blake "takes strong issue with the moral message Milton built into the masque."[19] He finds that in Blake's designs the issue of the choice which confronts the Lady offered the temptation of Comus is not at stake: "Triumph involves recognition of the contending elements as a prerequisite to the definitive choice. According to Blake's designs, the Lady achieves no such recognition and is consequently unable to make an informed choice."[20] The passivity of the Lady in Blake's pictures is what leads Behrendt to the conclusion, "She is not at all, in Blake's designs, an active participant in her Trial; she is merely *there*, paralyzed." I am going to argue now that a close look at certain illustrations from both sets of designs, with particular attention to dancing figures and changes of gesture in the characters, suggests that Behrendt is mistaken and that the seeming stasis of the Lady is "the magic of calm motion."[21]

Blake's first set of eight watercolours for *Comus*, executed in 1801 and now at the Huntington Library (here designated H) differs in important ways from his second set, executed circa 1815 for Thomas Butts and

99 Blake, *Comus*, plate 1 (H)

100 Blake, *Comus*, plate 1 (B)

101 Blake, *Comus*, plate 6 (H)

102 Blake, *Comus*, plate 6 (B)

now at the Boston Museum of Fine Arts (here designated B). Angus Fletcher defines the differences as an advance from "a theatricality in the first series to a more interior, more flowing drama in the second."[22] Irene Tayler, basing her discussion on the earlier H series only, suggests that Blake saw the action of the poem taking place in the theatre of the Lady's mind.[23] A close look at some of the details of Blake's changes bears out these observations and emphasizes also the important issue which Fletcher's essay on Milton's poem clarifies, the distinctions between chastity and virginity:

> ... here the most important distinction is that one can go on being chaste as long as one likes, but virginity (in its ideal essence, which is not to be confused with its merely physical aspect) suffers from entropy. Virginity at fifteen is more perfect than virginity at fifty ... virginity, like paradise, needs to be lost ... Chastity, on the other hand, is a ritually present, continuously rededicated ordering of the self ... In *Comus* it is the double of charity and thus has no beginning or end. It is the perfect instance of Christian temperance for both Spenser and Milton, since they are able to conceive of "married chastity."[24]

It is chastity that the Lady invokes, with faith, hope, and conscience, to protect her in the wood (lines 200 ff). How she is protected and what self-realization she comes to comprise the subject of Blake's designs.

In the first design of both sets (see figures 99 and 100) the composure of the Lady is a contrast to the energy of the ritual dance of Comus and his revellers. The dance is made more symmetrical and frieze-like in the B set, and the Lady's gesture changed to a gesture of protest. Behrendt mistakenly calls this a gesture of wonderment, but a comparison of this gesture with, say, *Job* 11, indicates protest. (In both sets, she sees Comus.) In *Comus* 2 (B) the palms of the hands are turned *upwards* to indicate wonder, and here too we see the attendant spirit making the gesture of protest as Comus in disguise approaches the Lady. Fletcher maintains that the second series is more "musical" than the first because in B "the actors adopt more dance-like, less agonistic postures than in H."[25] This assertion is borne out when the illustrations of the sixth design are compared (see figures 101 and 102). In B, both Comus and the brothers are more graceful in attitude, the symmetry of the brothers' stance suggesting simultaneity of movement as in a dance. Fletcher, of course, in calling a design "dance-like," is using this as a term of approbation. But we, by now, are wary of dance in Blake's designs and can perceive that the stillness of the Lady's posture (increased in effect by the change in her arm-position from across her breast to her lap) indicates that *her* activity is on another plane. As Irene Tayler saw, the cloud-effect around her suggests that this plane of action is her mind.

Fletcher regards Blake's designs as a proof that Blake perceived Milton's *Comus* as a "transcendental form,", that is, as a poetic structure which becomes a world of its own, transcending any formal limits or

103 Blake, *Comus*, plate 8 (B)

genre.[26] The added "radiance" of the second set – the subtle differences in use of light, the added rainbows of the final two designs – is an element of Fletcher's argument. I would add to his argument the transformation of the attendant spirit into a "leaping" figure of energy in 8 (B) (see figure 103): he is the visual symbol of her chastity. The elements of dance in these designs are subtle, but since we have seen the ambivalence which dancing suggests in other Blake designs, I think we must recognize that the appearance of passivity of the Lady in designs where others are moving with dance-like energy indicates constancy on her part rather than paralysis.

And now we return to our starting point, the significance of Albion's dance in *Albion Rose*. It was for the final state of the engraving (after 1803) that Blake added the inscription: "Albion rose from where he labourd at the Mill with Slaves / Giving himself for the Nations he danc'd the dance of Eternal Death"[27] (E 671). Robert Essick has brilliantly demonstrated that it was for this final state that the batwinged moth and segmented worm were also added.[28] This suggests to me that Blake was making explicit in both inscription and added images the darker implications of dance in his work. The tone of Essick's remarks emphasizes the regenerative nature of Albion's figure – and I do not wish to diminish that meaning (which I have remarked on in chapter 3), but I believe we cannot ignore that Albion is dancing a dance of *death*, albeit from motives of self-sacrifice.[29] Dance is a peculiarly *mortal* accomplishment in Blake's eyes, and in *Jerusalem* 76 it is what distinguishes Albion from the crucified Jesus.

When faced with this image, we are asked to consider the nature of death. Who in these pictures is truly alive? We may recall that in the design for *Milton* 15, when Milton is destroying Urizen's power, there are dancers with timbrels in Urizen's realm in the sky. A relevant comparison can be made with *Job* 14, *When the Morning Stars Sang Together*, which depicts a regenerate Jehovah whose angelic attendants are *standing still*. Can it be that stillness, not movement, is a sign of divinity?

Job and his family stand quietly with their musical instruments at the end of the series; Christ is often a passive figure in Blake's designs; both *Milton* and *Jerusalem* end with illustrations of stillness; only the leaping figure of Los's psychic energy in *J* 100 signifies a re-entry into the corporeal world, much as the passive Lady's attendant spirit leaps skywards in the final plate of *Comus*. We conclude, after surveying Blake's leaping and dancing figures in these chapters, that though mortal life may be a dance of death, the leap of psychic energy is a mode of transcendence.

COMMENTARY

The Fall of Man

Some of the meanings for figures and gestures I have been discussing will now be illustrated by a commentary on one of Blake's complicated watercolour designs, *The Fall of Man* (figure 104). The discussion here cannot be exhaustive – the subject alone can be said to cover the entire corpus of Blake's thought – but what can be demonstrated are insights and illuminations which aid in an understanding of Blake's intent and result in an interpretation of the picture.

This design, executed in 1807, is a companion to the watercolour *A Vision of the Last Judgment* (figure 105), dated 1806. The pictures form a pair of theological commentaries which sum up Blake's concerns at the time. The *Last Judgment* is a subject to which Blake kept returning in watercolours, drawings, two prose manuscripts, and an immense lost fresco.[1] *The Fall of Man*, however, is known to us only in this one design and seems a subject rather more manageable in a synoptic picture meant to capture a moment and all its effects. Blake must have been writing and revising *The Four Zoas* at the time he worked on this watercolour, and he had already conceived *Milton* and *Jerusalem*, as we know from the dates of 1804 on their title-pages, so the subject of the Fall was very much in his mind. In the same year in which he executed this design, he also produced his first set of illustrations to *Paradise Lost* (now the Huntington Library set), to be followed the next year by the large set for Thomas Butts (Boston Museum of Fine Arts). We will find connections and visual quotations shared among these works.

The Fall of Man is a pen-and-watercolour design. It is signed "1807 W Blake inv"; on the back in copper-plate hand is written:

The Father indignant at the Fall – the Savior, while the Evil Angels are driven, gently conducts our first Parents out of Eden through a Guard of Weeping Angels – Satan now awakes Sin, Death, & Hell, to celebrate with him the birth of War & Misery: while the Lion seizes the Bull, the Tiger the Horse, the Vulture and the Eagle contend for the Lamb & c.[2]

104 Blake, *The Fall of Man*

105 Blake, *A Vision of the Last Judgment*

If we begin at the top of the picture, we see a bearded patriarch, "the Father," whom we recognize as a Urizenic figure in the familiar outstretched-arm pose (recalling *America* 8). He is surrounded by twelve spirits above in clouds, one with a small scroll inscribed with the letters INRI ("Jesus of Nazareth, King of the Jews"). The scroll-carrying spirit and his counterpart are each in the leaping pose of energy figures. Four other figures, two on each side, complete the Father's retinue: on his left, one figure with a flaming sword holds out a goblet; on his right, one with a spear holds out a plate with a round loaf of bread (these are symbols of the harvest and vintage of eternity). Two semi-recumbent figures complete the circle: one, on the patriarch's left, also with flaming sword, receives nails; the other, on his right, receives a thorn. Thus are present all the symbols of the Crucifixion, in motion, as if being decreed at that moment by Jehovah.

Simultaneously, in the centre of the picture, immediately beneath the Father, a flame-enveloped figure with a sword strangles with his left hand the Serpent wrapped around the thorny apple-bearing Tree of Knowledge. Another fruit-bearing tree stands on his right, and between the trees is a vista of the Garden of Eden. Four other figures, two on each side, complete the symmetry of the top part of the picture: on each side, one figure carries a sword and one a spear and shield. They are attending to the falling figures ("Evil Angels") which careen down each side of the picture amid flames and lightning. A number of the falling figures are in head-clutching attitudes of despair or have their arms and hands thrown up, indicating astonishment. One, at the left-hand margin near the bottom, raises his hands and eyes in admiration, even as he falls. These are the rebel angels being cast out of Heaven. Blake conflates here with the Expulsion an event which, according to Milton, preceded the Fall of Adam and Eve. He is able to indicate, by their poses, the psychological states of the angels as they fall.

In the upper half of both sides of the picture are three peculiar bubbles, the centre bubble containing a figure sketched in a huddle-pose of despair; a large bubble on the right contains a figure in flight, while the figure in the large left bubble appears to be pushing against its sides. Blake has used bubbles in other designs – for example, in *Mirth* (figure 97). They seem to me to suggest the existence of other worlds or, perhaps, other states of being. In this case, all other worlds are affected negatively by the event of the Fall.

In the centre of the picture are the figures of Adam and Eve led out of Paradise by Christ, over whose head is hovering the Dove, Christian symbol of the Holy Spirit. Christ also has a star-shaped halo. When Blake illustrated this Expulsion for *Paradise Lost*, he pictured Michael escorting Adam and Eve, as Milton did (figure 106). It is most unusual to have Christ present at the Fall;[3] Blake emphasizes by this that the Fall and Redemption are simultaneous. It is significant that neither Adam nor Eve wears a fig-leaf, symbol of their shame and fall, as they do in the

Paradise Lost design. Thus, their redemption is further emphasized. The figure of Christ is in the "Apollo" form Blake tends to use for moments which reveal the true identity of a figure (recall *Milton*, plate 16).[4] Eve is a figure of Dejection after LeBrun (see chapter 2), but Adam is not at all broken: he is apparently engaged in conversation; his head is turned to Jesus, and one hand is raised in a gesture of admiration. This is a Blakean touch of characterization.

106 Blake, *Paradise Lost: Expulsion from Eden*

Behind Adam, Eve, and Christ are some curious horizontal lines, perhaps indicating a barrier from Eden. At their feet is the demonstration that all nature has fallen – the animals begin to prey upon each other ("The Lion seizes the Bull, the Tiger the Horse ...").

The lower third of the picture illustrates the underworld, where "Satan now awakes Sin, Death, & Hell to celebrate with him the birth of War & Misery." Satan stands at the bottom-left of the design, rousing his legions in an upward-pointing pose that we recognize as prophetic (compare Elihu in *Job* 12). His body, like those of Adam and Eve and, indeed, some of the fallen angels, is a sublime nude, not yet tainted by the Fall. His pose is prophetic because, though chronologically he raises his legions *before* the fall of Adam and Eve, here he indicates what is happening to them; Blake is picturing these events simultaneously and giving Satan a knowledge of the future that he does not have in Milton. Interestingly, Death looks like the Father and is in a similar outstretched-arm pose of power and thwarted creativity (see chapter 3): this is a convention Blake will use again in the *Job* designs to emphasize the relationship between Job and his God. Here Death has a crown on his head, while the Father has hair which looks like horns: these are details which further emphasize a connection between the two. The expressions on the faces of Jehovah and Death are similar, though varying in intensity. Surprisingly, in spite of the words on the back of the painting, the Father does *not* look "Indignant"; he resembles LeBrun's depictions of sadness (see figure 25), as if he is decreeing the Fall more in sorrow than in anger. Death, as he gestures towards Sin (another female) appears to express Pain (also after LeBrun). The other attributes of Sin and Death are those Blake uses throughout the *Paradise Lost* designs and will continue to use in *Jerusalem*: Death has jagged bat-like wings, like the Spectre in *J* 6; Sin is accompanied by flames and serpents (she is not the half-serpent she becomes in *Paradise Lost*).

The sleeping woman on Death's left is, I would suggest, Vala, or Fallen Nature, who is not roused by the Fall but rather put to sleep. Her sword is sinking, and her goblet, symbol of the vintage of eternity, is tilted over in her hand. Her wings are curved and moth-like, recalling Leutha, daughter of Satan in Blake's *Milton* 11 (line 36; E 105). She is accompanied by a grazing horse and a ram. Both of these beasts have a place in the Apocalypse: the horses pull the chariot of the redeemed Urizen in *Job* 14, and the ram is a symbol of innocence.[5] Beneath Sin, Death, and Vala emerge the armies of "War and Misery."

After examining the details of this picture, one comes away considering certain very Blakean implications. The first is that the Fall *was* the Expulsion. The leaving of Eden and not the disobedience of Adam and Eve is the moment at which Nature falls and Hell awakes. (We might remember that Blake has suggested this once before, in the title-page to *Songs of Innocence and of Experience*, where an Expulsion scene suggests the state of Experience.) Certainly, in the history of the iconography of the Fall of man in Western art, this picture is astonishingly original. While it is usual to suggest redemption and perhaps judgment in Christian art which portrays the Fall, the usual visual formula concerns the moment of the taking of the apple,[6] not the Expulsion.

From this observation, the question arises: who caused the Expulsion? According to the picture, the Father decrees the Expulsion; he has judged that Adam and Eve have to go. In other words, a moral judgment, a Urizenic act, is the Fall.[7] This insight helps to explain why Blake would have Jehovah and Death appear as twins in this design; it also illuminates the twin appearance of Job and Jehovah in the *Job* designs: Job's fall is brought about by *his* Urizenic behaviour, continually following the "letter" of the Hebraic code.[8] Here, Death is the counterpart of the Father, the dark side of a Urizenic god, who initiates Time, and therefore Death, by expelling Adam and Eve. The Fall of man is the Fall of God.

In many ways, Time is the sub-text of this design. The symmetry of figures in the composition is almost too careful, and there are three neat levels of action: Heaven, Earth, and Hell. But this symmetry provides a stability for the frenetic action within the design: flames, lightning, falling figures, beast attacking beast. There is also a suggestion of a cacaphony of sound: where there is lightning, there must be thunder; mouths are open for screams; angels weep. And all this happens *in one moment*, when past and future merge. Adam and Eve are expelled and redeemed at the same time: in that moment, Christ has entered the fallen world and the Crucifixion is decreed. Sin and Death awake. Nature falls asleep, and Time begins.

Conclusion

In this book my principal concern has been to demonstrate that a visual language exists in Blake's designs which can reinforce our understanding of them and often illuminate the ideas of the texts they illustrate. When Blake uses his tremendous visionary clichés, he is affirming in visual terms his aphorism of *The Ghost of Abel*: "Nature has no Outline: but Imagination has" (E 270). The human form *in art*, in other words, is what is worthy of attention, for the filter of the human imagination is what turns a foggy natural form into an artistic one. Once established, and therefore copied over the years by generations of artists, the visual image of the human body in a familiar pose is an Eternal Form in Blake's eyes, part of a visual language available to all.

Can there be a dictionary to Blake's language of art? As in all Blakean questions, the answer must be qualified. The issue always comes down to this: what does the context do to the form in question? My answer usually is: context points us in the direction of the meaning. As we have seen, there is a nucleus of images of the human body, often first used with established meanings in the *Night Thoughts* designs, which Blake continuously relies on over the years until in the *Job* designs they reappear as a confirmation of his visual vocabulary. When Blake uses one of these images – particularly the outstretched arms and the despair and energy figures discussed in this book – we can be assured of a kernel of meaning which the context will elaborate for us.

In our attempts to understand *how* Blake's designs mean, we are led into the mysterious labyrinths of the interactions between word and image. W.J.T. Mitchell claims an *independence* of design from text in order that a "marriage of equals" can take place; yet words consistently dominate Blake's designs, whether they are actually engraved on a plate, as in the illuminated books or the *Job* series, or implied because the design illustrates another writer's poem, as in *Comus*. Verbal meanings are not isolated in their own realm, able to maintain one side of a dialectic; they are attached to the visual image from the beginning because of traditions of iconography or mime. In Norman Bryson's illuminating recent study of French painting in the eighteenth century, *Word and Image*, the author states:

> We have not yet found ourselves able to dispense altogether in our dealings with the image with some form of contact with language. And language enormously shapes and delimits our reception of images.[1]

This principle Blake appears to have recognized early and built into his work, sometimes using the same image in different poetic contexts, thus making subtle links between them even as our perception is reshaped.

When one artist "borrows" a motif from another, art historians use the term *quotation*, suggesting the linguistic analogy we instinctively bring from verbal to visual images. Blake likes to quote himself, emphasizing thereby these links. Of course, as we have seen, Blake quoting himself is often Blake quoting another source too. David Bindman, writing on "Blake's Theory and Practice of Imitation," outlines the widespread practice of Blake and his contemporaries of using classical formula-figures: "These artists did not regard borrowing as shameful, but on the contrary they wore the badge of imitation with pride."[2]

Bindman suggests that Blake remains a classical idealist even after he turns away from Greek art and literature: "Blake's attitudes toward art are in a profound sense eighteenth century in spirit ..."[3] Yet as I have tried to demonstrate, Blake's mode of imitation attempted to transcend the limits of copying, to produce instead re-creations, using the pictorial language the past had provided. The images then function as keystones or directional signs, aids to an understanding of Blake's own multi-dimensional texts. It is not as a classical idealist that Blake claims our attention but as a modern innovator. Blake's friend George Cumberland summed up a lifetime of collecting Italian engravings in these words:

> It is not to steal the ideas of the old masters that we study them, but rather to amalgamate them with those of each other and our own: new ideas of beauty and grandeur can alone arise from happy combinations, and as he that has read attentively the best Authors is likely to acquire the best style, so he that is conversant with the works of all the good Artists, it is most likely, will be successful in his own.[4]

Blake would have approved of the concept of new, beautiful, and grand ideas arising from "happy combinations"; they are the result of participation in the world of images:

> If the Spectator could Enter into these Images in his Imagination approaching them on the Fiery Chariot of his Contemplative Thought if he could Enter into Noahs Rainbow or into his bosom or could make a Friend & Companion of one of these Images of wonder which always intreats him to leave mortals things as he must know then would he arise from his Grave then would he meet the Lord in the Air & then he would be happy. (E 560)

Notes

PREFACE

1 W.J.T. Mitchell, *Blake's Composite Art* (Princeton: Princeton University Press 1978), 58.

INTRODUCTION: A HERITAGE OF IMAGES

1 From the advertisement for *A Descriptive Catalogue of Blake's Exhibition*, in *The Complete Poetry and Prose of William Blake*, ed. David V. Erdman (Berkeley and Los Angeles: University of California Press 1982), 528. (Hereinafter, this edn. will be referred to as E.)
2 *Descriptive Catalogue*, E 542. See also G.E. Bentley, Jr, *Blake Records* (Oxford: Clarendon 1969), 222, n. 1.
3 For detailed background, see David V. Erdman, *Blake: Prophet Against Empire*, 3rd edn. (Princeton: Princeton University Press 1977), especially chap. 26.
4 *Annotations to Reynolds*, E 636.
5 *Milton* 1 (hereinafter referred to as *M*), E 95.
6 Ibid.
7 "It is the Classics! & not Goths nor Monks, that Desolate Europe with Wars" (*On Homer's Poetry*, E 270).
8 Letter to the editor of the *Monthly Magazine*, July 1806 (E 768).
9 "Public Address," E 582.
10 Bo Lindberg's excellent study, *William Blake's Illustrations to the Book of Job* (Abo, Finland: Abo Akademi 1973), recognizes the language of art I deal with and shares similar opinions on its importance for Blake.
11 We are particularly indebted to the work of the eminent art historians Saxl, Seznec, Panofsky, Gombrich, Praz, Wind, and Rosenblum for this background. See especially Fritz Saxl, *A Heritage of Images: A Selection of Lectures by Fritz Saxl* (Harmondsworth: Penguin 1970), and the *Lectures* first published by the Warburg Institute (London 1957); E. Wind, *Pagan Mys-*

teries in The Renaissance* (New Haven: Yale University Press 1958); Jean Seznec, *The Survival of the Pagan Gods* (New York: Harper Torchbook 1961), originally published in French as *La Survivance dex dieux antiques*, Studies of the Warburg Institute XI (1940); Erwin Panofsky, *Studies in Iconology* (1939; New York: Harper 1962); Dora and Erwin Panofsky, *Pandora's Box: The Changing Aspects of a Mythical Symbol* (New York: Pantheon 1962); E.H. Gombrich, *Symbolic Images* (Oxford: Phaidon 1972); Mario Praz, *Studies in Seventeenth-Century Imagery* (London: Warburg 1939); Robert Rosenblum, *Transformations in Late Eighteenth-Century Art* (Princeton: Princeton University Press 1967).

12 Seznec, *Survival of the Pagan Gods*, 278.

13 See Jean H. Hagstrum, *William Blake, Poet and Painter* (Chicago: University of Chicago Press 1964), chap. 4, and David V. Erdman, *The Notebook of William Blake* (Oxford: Clarendon 1973). Judith Wardle discusses emblem history in an unpublished essay from which I have learned a great deal.

14 Piloo Nanavutty, "Blake and Emblem Literature," *Journal of the Warburg and Courtauld Institute* 15 (1952): 261.

15 *Annotations to Reynolds*, E 644.

16 Anthony Blunt, *The Art of William Blake* (New York: Columbia University Press 1959), 41.

17 This is not to say that these artists did not sometimes concern themselves with priorities. Fuseli is reputed to have said, "Blake is damned good to steal from," and Blake wrote in his "Public Address": "Flaxman cannot deny that one of the very first Monuments he did I gratuitously designed for him ... how much of his Homer & Dante he will allow to be mine I do not know as he went far enough off to Publish them even to Italy. but the Public will know & Posterity will know" (E 572). See also the *Notebook* lines "To Nancy F—," "How can I help thy Husbands copying Me / Should that make difference twixt me & Thee" (E 507).

18 Joseph Burke, "The Eidetic and the Borrowed Image: An Interpretation of Blake's Theory and Practice of Art," reprinted in *The Visionary Hand*, ed. Robert N. Essick (Los Angeles: Hennessey and Ingalls 1973), 253.

19 Rosenblum, *Transformations*, figs. 184–7. Rosenblum sees in the phenomenon a new attitude to the historical past, termed *historicism*, reflected in the re-creation of a documentary past on canvas. Frederick Antal, in *Fuseli Studies* (London: Routledge 1956), notes that Fuseli repeats himself: "In some of the innumerable drawings, and even more in the pictures, the composition, as well as the attitudes of individual figures, tends to repeat rather monotonously certain fixed formulae. Unrealistic artists necessarily systematise in their compositions more than those whose art is continually fed and rejuvenated by studies after nature" (91). In a note Antal further observes: "Such a repetition of formulae also occurs in the greater, equally stylising artist, Blake" (111).

20 See Irwin Panofsky, *Idea: A Concept in Art Theory* (Columbia: University of South Carolina Press 1968); and Annabel M. Patterson, "Tasso and Neoplatonism," *Studies in the Renaissance* XVII (1971).

21 George Mills Harper, *The Neoplatonism of William Blake* (Chapel Hill: University of North Carolina Press 1961), 35.

22 E.H. Gombrich, *Symbolic Images* (London: Phaidon 1972), 123.

23 E.H. Gombrich, "Icones Symbolicae. The Visual Image in Neo-Platonic Thought," *JWCI* (1948): 168. This is the first version of the final chapter of *Symbolic Images*.

24 C. Giarda, *Bibliotheca Alexandrinae Icones Symbolicae*, reproduced in G. Graevius and P. Burmannus, *Thesaurus Antiquitatum* (1725). A copy of Graevius was in the original British Museum Catalogue. Giarda's introduction is reproduced in Gombrich's *Symbolic Images*.

25 Translated by Gombrich, *Symbolic Images*, 154.

26 The bitter controversy concerning the *engraving* of these designs not by Blake but by Schiavonetti is well known. See G.E. Bentley, Jr, "Blake and Cromek: The Wheat and the Tares," *Journal of Modern Philology* 71, no. 4 (May 1974): 366 ff. My excerpt is taken from Bentley's article.

27 This was the basis of the emblem tradition at its best.

28 See Northrop Frye, *Fearful Symmetry* (Princeton: Princeton University Press 1947), 25.

29 There are various versions of this myth, but the version known to Blake was probably from Ovid's *Metamorphoses*.

30 Mentioned by Kenneth Clark, *The Nude in Art* (Harmondsworth: Penguin 1969), 404. For a complete account of the source of this image see Francis Haskell and Nicholas Penny, *Taste and the Antique* (New Haven: Yale University Press 1981), "Cleopatra," 184–7.

31 Geoffrey Keynes, *Blake Studies* (London: Rupert Hart-Davies 1949), 68–9.

32 From "A Humanist Dreamland" (1945), in Saxl, *A Heritage of Images*.

ONE: BLAKE'S METAPHORS OF FORM

1 Anne K. Mellor, *Blake's Human Form Divine* (Berkeley: University of California Press 1974).

2 Anyone who explores this topic is indebted to George Mills Harper, *The Neoplatonism of William Blake* (Chapel Hill: University of North Carolina Press 1961), especially chaps. 6 and 7, "The Ideal Forms" and "The Absence of Forms." Even when one disagrees with some of Harper's arguments, one is grateful for a clear and stimulating expression of difficult ideas.

3 Jean H. Hagstrum, "Christ's Body," in *William Blake: Essays in Honour of Sir Geoffrey Keynes*, ed. Morton D. Paley and Michael Phillips (Oxford: Clarendon 1973), 130.

4 Harper, *Neoplatonism of Blake*, 271.

5 Peter Fisher, *The Valley of Vision* (Toronto: University of Toronto Press 1961), 48.

6 Harper, *Neoplatonism of Blake*, 92.

7 In this context, these lines refer to the appearance of the real and eternal forms of the earth.

8 See FZ I: 5; E 303. Blake does not appear to have used the shadow-Spectre connection before *The Four Zoas*. The Covering Cherub is derived from Ezek. 28:14–16.

9 See Morton D. Paley's important article, "The Figure of the Garment in *The Four Zoas*, *Milton* and *Jerusalem*," in *Blake's Sublime Allegory*, ed. S. Curran and J. Wittreich, Jr (Madison: University of Wisconsin Press 1973), 119–39.

10 Ibid., 131.

11 Ibid., 138.

12 Thomas R. Frosch, *The Awakening of Albion* (Ithaca: Cornell University Press 1974), 10. See also 44–50, for an excellent account of the creation of the body.

13 See I Cor. 12:12, 15:44.

14 Samuel Johnson's *Dictionary* defines *chaos* primarily as "the mass of matter supposed to be in confusion before it was divided by the creation into its proper classes and elements."

15 I note in chap. 4 the combination of rage, lust, and pride at the birth of Tharmas's spectre and how he goes on to experience with Enion all the seven deadly sins.

16 For another aspect of Thel's radiance, see the important article by Christopher Heppner, "A Desire of Being: Identity and the Book of Thel," *Colby Library Quarterly* XXIII (June 1977): 81. Heppner believes that Thel's similes reveal "the apparently ungraspable nature of her identity," reflecting a background of discussion in the eighteenth century on the problem of personal identity.

TWO: THE VISUAL LANGUAGE OF THE PASSIONS

1 See Brewster Rogerson, "The Art of Painting the Passions," *Journal of the History of Ideas* 14 (1953): 68–94. Also very useful is the introduction by Alan T. McKenzie to the Augustan Reprint Society's edition of Charles LeBrun, *A Method to Learn to Design the Passions* (1734; William Andrews Clark Memorial Library, UCLA 1980).

2 McKenzie, intro. to LeBrun, *A Method*, iii.

3 For a longer discussion of Blake's ideas of copying and the distinctions he makes between imitation and invention, see chap. 1.

4 LeBrun, *A Method*, 48. For historical background on LeBrun's career, see McKenzie's intro., iii.

5 Gerard de Lairesse, *The Art of Painting* (London 1738), 55. See also Alastair Smart, "Dramatic Gesture and Expression in the Age of Hogarth and Reynolds," *Apollo* 82 (1965): 90–7.

6 In the Huntington Library; reproduced in Martin Butlin, *The Paintings and Drawings of William Blake* (New Haven and London: Yale University Press 1981), *Plates*, 1126–77. (Hereinafter, this edn. will be referred to as Butlin.)

7 *For the Curious* (London: B. Dickinson 1751). Lens's long title is virtually identical to the subtitle of Lairesse's *The Principles of Design*. This work was published without Mr Lens's additions (mostly landscapes and perspective views) in London in 1777.

8 "Public Address," E 577.

9 McKenzie, intro. to LeBrun, *A Method*, v.

10 Rogerson, "Art of Painting the Passions," 75.

11 McKenzie provides a concise account of these terms:

> The "concupiscible" passions have as their "objects" (or stimuli) simple and attainable good or avoidable evil either present, future or possessed. Thus, present good = Love, and evil = Hate, future good = Desire, and evil = Loathing; and possessed good = Joy, and evil = Sadness. The second category contains the "irascible" passions, those which have remoter objects and are attainable or avoidable only with some difficulty. They are Hope, Despair, Courage, Fear, and Anger (*Summa Theologiae*, I, 81; II, 24–48). These eleven basic passions can combine to produce others. Love and Hate, for example, combine to produce either Envy or Jealousy, depending on whether the loved object is desired or possessed. This system, if it can be called that, prevailed well into the eighteenth century ... (intro. to LeBrun, *A Method*, v)

12 For an excellent account, see Smart, "Dramatic Gesture," 93 ff.

13 See chap. 3 below, or my article "Blake's Use of Gesture: The Outstretched Arms," in *Blake's Visionary Forms Dramatic*, ed. David V. Erdman and John E. Grant (Princeton: Princeton University Press 1970), 174–95.

14 The margin of the watercolour in the Huntington Library is inscribed "Acts IX C 6V."

15 Bo Lindberg, *William Blake's Illustrations to the Book of Job* (Abo, Finland: Abo Akademi 1973), 116.

16 Such copying had even been advocated by C.A. DuFresnoy in *Observations on the Art of Painting*, a treatise first published in France in 1695 and translated by John Dryden. It was widely known, and a version in heroic couplets with lengthy notes by Joshua Reynolds was published in 1783. DuFresnoy wrote:

> These passions (as I have said) ought to be learnt from the Life itself, or to be studied on the Ancient Statues, and excellent Pictures: we ought to see, for Example, all things which belong to Sadness, or serve to express it; to design them carefully, and to imprint them in our memories after such a Manner, as we may distinctly understand seven or eight kinds of them more or less, and immediately after draw them on Paper, without any other Original, than the Image which we have conceiv'd of them. (158)

While Blake would always rail against using the faculty of memory to produce generalities ("To generalize is to be an Idiot"), he would approve of DuFresnoy's advocation to observe "seven or eight kinds" of distinctly understood expressions of sadness.

17 See John Graham, *Lavater's Essays on Physiognomy: A Study in the History of Ideas* (Berne: Peter Lang 1979). See also Anne K. Mellor, "Physiognomy,

Phrenology, and Blake's Visionary Heads," in *Blake in His Time*, ed. Robert N. Essick and Donald Pearce (Bloomington: Indiana University Press 1978), 53–74.

18 See Peter Tomory, *The Life and Art of Henry Fuseli* (London: Thames and Hudson 1972).

19 John Caspar Lavater, *Essays in Physiognomy* trans. Henry Hunter, 3 vols. in 5 (London: J. Murray 1789–98), vol. I, 27.

20 Ibid., author's preface.

21 Ibid., vol. II, 89.

22 An annotated and clarified edition of *Chirologia ... Chironomia*, the first in three centuries, has been edited by James W. Cleary (Southern Illinois University Press 1974). Cleary's introduction and notes are indispensable. I have consulted for my research the *Chirologia* in the Osler Library at McGill University and in the William Andrews Clark Memorial Library at UCLA. Page references will be made here to Cleary's edition, which is more accessible to scholars than an original. I am heavily indebted to Cleary's introduction for the background sketch which follows.

23 Cleary, intro. to Bulwer, *Chirologia ... Chironomia*, xxx–xxxiv.

24 *Observations on the Art of Painting*, 162.

25 See also below, chap. 3, or its original appearance as "Blake's Use of Gesture," 185–7, where I suggest that the detail of hand design becomes more consistent as Blake's art develops.

26 Cleary, intro. to Bulwer, *Chirologia ... Chironomia*, xxxiv–xxxv.

27 Ibid., xx.

28 Bulwer, *Chirologia ... Chironomia*, 188.

29 Ibid., 21.

30 Ibid., 23.

31 Lindberg, *Blake's Illustrations to Job*, 213.

32 While I am arguing about details here, I am not disputing Lindberg's assertion that Job's entire seated attitude is based on formula-figures of other art Blake could have known.

33 Quintilian, "Manus sinistra nanquam sua gestum recte facit." Cited in Cleary, intro. to Bulwer, *Chirologia ... Chironomia*, xxxiv.

34 Bulwer, *Chirologia ... Chironomia*, 42.

35 See G.E. Bentley, Jr, ed., *Tiriel* facsimile (Oxford: Clarendon 1967), plate V, 39.

36 *Tiriel*, line 66; E 281.

37 See Bentley, *Tiriel*, plate VI; and Warner, "Blake's Use of Gesture," 189. The positive use of this gesture is "Blessing"; see *Job* 17.

38 Lindberg, *Blake's Illustrations to Job*, 241.

39 Bulwer, *Chirologia ... Chironomia*, 49 and 208 (gesture of adoration).

40 See also Lindberg, *Blake's Illustrations to Job*, 241.

41 Warner, "Blake's Use of Gesture," 179, and below, chap. 3.

42 Bulwer, *Chirologia ... Chironomia*, 187.

43 There are, however, important changes of direction involved. Job sits on the left, the friends on the right. In the engraving their positions are reversed.

44 The engravings show surprisingly little variation from the watercolours. One other significant change I have found is with *Job* 20, where in the engraving Job's fingers are changed into the "creative" fingers to suggest his awakened vision (noted in "Blake's Use of Gesture," 186).

45 See Butlin, *Text*, 113. David Erdman believes that these drawings are copies by Rosetti of Blake's designs.

46 Alastair Smart, "Dramatic Gesture and Expression in the Age of Hogarth and Reynolds," *Apollo* 82 (1965): 90.

47 Emma actually became the wife of Sir William Hamilton in 1791.

48 Brian Reade, *Ballet Designs and Illustrations 1581–1940* (London: Victoria and Albert Museum 1967), intro.

49 Friedrich Rehberg, *Lady Hamilton's Attitudes* (London: S.W. Fores 1797). The drawings were made at Naples in 1794, and the engravings for the book were done by Tommasso Piroli.

50 Album of outlines by George Cumberland in the British Museum Print Room (201 c. 1).

51 P.A. Tomory *The Life and Art of Henry Fuseli* (London: Thames and Hudson 1972), 165. The excerpt is from Tomory's section entitled "Symbolic Anatomy," which comments also on dismembered anatomy and the knees and forelegs in Fuseli's work – all of which may be relevant to his influence on Blake.

52 Betterton, *The History of the English Stage*, 73.

53 Thomas Wilkes, *A General View of the English Stage* (London 1759), 95; Thomas Betterton, *The History of the English Stage* (London 1741), 87.

54 Noted by Smart, "Dramatic Gesture," 93.

55 Obadiah Walker, *The Art of Oratory* (London 1659), 127.

56 For background, see Alan S. Downer, "Nature to Advantage Dressed: Eighteenth-Century Acting," PMLA LVIII (Dec. 1943): 1002–37.

57 See Irene Tayler, *Blake's Illustrations to the Poems of Gray* (Princeton: Princeton University Press 1971).

58 See *William Blake's Designs for Edward Young's Night Thoughts*, ed. David V. Erdman, John E. Grant, Edward J. Rose, Michael J. Tolley, 2 vols. (Oxford: Clarendon 1980).

59 David Mayer III, *Harlequin in His Element, The English Pantomime 1806–1836* (Cambridge, Mass.: Harvard University Press 1969).

60 Marian Hannah Winter, *The Pre-Romantic Ballet* (London: Pitman 1974), 178.

61 John Weaver, *The History of the Mimes and Pantomimes with an Historical Account of several Performers in Dancing, living in the Time of the Roman Emperors*. The sub-title adds "... A List of the Modern Entertainments that have been exhibited on the *English* stage, either in Imitation of the ancient *Pantomimes* or after the manner of the Modern *Italians*; when and where first Performed, and by whom composed" (London 1728). Weaver had previously written the first attempt at dance history in England in his *Essay towards a History of Dancing* (London 1712).

62 John Weaver, *The Loves of Mars and Venus* (London 1717). Much of this passage can be found in Winter, *The Pre-Romantic Ballet*, 58–60.

63 To complete this survey of visual languages available to Blake, it is necessary to mention the art of *writing* dancing, or methods of recording dance movement. Some of these works, although often difficult to follow, could have been known to Blake, and they emphasize for us the eighteenth century's desire to record and categorize in all the arts. R.A. Feuillet's *Choreography, or the Art of Writing Dancing* (1701) appeared in English in 1782 and Pierre Rameau's *Maître à Danser* (1725) in 1731. Earlier, social dances had been described by T. Arbeau in *Orchesographie* (1588) and John Playford's *The English Dancing Master* (1650). From these books we can, for instance, trace the evolution of the "five positions" of the feet. It was the famous teacher Carlo Blasis (1797–1878) who codified in 1820 what were the traditional ballet movements of the times, with drawings of the human figure, in his *Elementary Treatise upon the Theory and Practice of the Art of Dancing*, published first in Italy and then in England, Denmark, and Spain within months. Blasis's later work, the *Code of Terpsichore*, was written and published first in English in 1829 and became the standard reference for dance instruction in Europe and Russia.

APPENDIX: THE DOMESTIC IMAGES

1 Ian Maxted, *The London Book Trades, 1775–1800: A Preliminary Check List of Members* (Folkestone: Dawson 1944), table 3, xxii.
2 David V. Erdman, *Blake: Prophet Against Empire*, 3rd edn. (Princeton: Princeton University Press 1977), 90.
3 A set of porcelain figures has been found to have been directly inspired by a series of nineteenth century prints. See Alwyn and Angela Cox, "Hippolyte LeComte and the Rockingham peasant figures," *The Connoisseur* (July 1977).
4 See *English Printed Textiles* (London: Victoria and Albert Museum 1960), 2. Some of the material in this section has also appeared in my article "Blake and English Printed Textiles," *Blake Newsletter* (Spring 1973).
5 Alexander Gilchrist, *Life of William Blake* (London: Everyman 1945), 28. See also p. 49 for a reference to Trotter's own paintings.
6 See John Irwin and Katharine B. Brett, *Origins of Chintz* (London: Victoria and Albert Museum 1970).
7 The volume constitutes the pattern-book of Foster & Co of the Bromley Hall works (Poplar, Middlesex, ca. 1760–1800); in the Victoria and Albert Museum.
8 Barbara J. Morris, "English Printed Textiles: v. Sports and Pastimes," *Antiques* 62 (Sept. 1951): 253. This is one of nine articles by Peter Flood and Barbara Morris on English eighteenth-century copper-plate textiles and early nineteenth-century roller prints, *Antiques*, March 1957 to April 1958.
9 Reproduced in Ruthven Todd, *William Blake the Artist* (London: Studio Vista 1971), 26.

10 A decorative process for which English must take full credit (or blame) was that of transfer-printing. Here all the artistry went into the engraving of a copper-plate, which was then inked with an enamel-like pigment and from which an indefinite number of paper transfers could be taken for application to the wares and subsequent firing in the enamel-kiln. The process, originating probably in the Battersea enamel factory after 1753, was probably taken after 1756 successively to Bow and Worcester by the engraver Robert Hancock.

From R.J. Charleston, ed., *English Porcelain 1745–1850* (Toronto: University of Toronto Press 1965), 19.

11 Todd, *Blake the Artist*, 102–3. Todd reproduces a page of the catalogue.

12 See G.E. Bentley, Jr, *Blake Records* (Oxford: Clarendon 1969), 239–41, for correspondence.

PART TWO: FOUR FIGURES

1 Northrop Frye, *Anatomy of Criticism: Four Essays* (Princeton: Princeton University Press 1957), 365.

THREE: HUMANITY DIVINE

1 The pencil sketches are dated 1780 because the signature on the engraved *Albion Rose* reads "W B inv 1780," though the plate was not engraved until the 1790s.

2 Anthony Blunt, *The Art of William Blake* (New York: Columbia University Press 1959), 34. Blunt's first discussion of Blake's sources for this picture, calling attention to the Scamozzi figure, appeared in the *Journal of the Warburg & Courtauld Institutes* II (1938): 65–8.

3 It is a Renaissance example of Vitruvian man, used to demonstrate that the proportions of the human body are the ideal pattern for architecture and design. Desiree Hirst (*Hidden Riches* [New York: Barnes & Noble 1964], 53–4) points out that Blake was also probably familiar with Agrippa's Vitruvian figures.

4 Engraved in 1793; the later additions of 1818 include the key for this plate: "Holy & cold, I clipd the Wings of all Sublunary Things." The association of repressive authority with a bearded old man occurred earlier, in Blake's drawings for *Tiriel*, which represent the tyrannical king as a bearded patriarch. Tiriel is never shown in the specific poses I am discussing, although he is pictured raising one arm to curse.

5 Robert E. Gleckner, *The Piper and the Bard* (Detroit: Wayne State University Press 1959), 193.

6 Blunt (p. 41) has suggested the figure of Jupiter Pluvius in a Roman relief as the source of this motif, tracing its appearance in the work of Blake, Flaxman, and Romney and finding Blake's first use in his Nile engraving of 1791, after Fuseli. The earlier *All Religions Are One* figure, however, does seem to be the same except for its lack of wings.

7 *NT* 27. The text illustrated in Night I, lines 315–43, supports this interpretation. Words evoking the snake images – "rises," "sting," "envenomd," "beware," "death" – are collocated with abstractions – "rises" with "misfortune," "sting" with "distress," "envenomd" with "rage" and "peace," "beware" with "happiness," "death" with "joys." Thus we are invited to see the serpent-wrapped dead man as representative of a mental state.

8 E.J. Rose has described and commented on hand positions in "Blake's Hand: Symbol and Design in *Jerusalem*," *Texas Studies in Literature and Language* IV (1965): 48–9.

FOUR: FIGURES OF DESPAIR

1 Some indication of the frequency of these repeated images in Blake's designs can be demonstrated by the following list, which is by no means exhaustive:
HUDDLED, FRONT VIEW: *Jerusalem* 41, 51; *America*, frontispiece, 1; *Vala* I: 5; *Gates of Paradise* 4, 16; *Urizen*, passim; *Job* 12; *VDA*, frontispiece, 4, 8; *Hecate*; *Dante* 3; *NT*, passim.
BENT-OVER, SIDE VIEW: *America* 16; *Europe* 5; *Vala* VIIB: 96; *Job* 6 and passim; *NT* 19, 28, and frequently.
FALLING: *A Vision of the Last Judgment*; *America* 5; *Urizen* 6; *Spiritual Form of Nelson Guiding Leviathan*; *Job* 16.
PROSTRATE: *Job* 6 and 11; *Jerusalem* 94, 33, 63; *Lazar House*; *Vala* VIIA: 78.

2 I use the terms *deadly sins* and *cardinal sins* interchangeably, as is usual in modern terminology, to refer to pride, wrath, envy, avarice, sloth, gluttony, and lust. (This is the Gregorian list which Dante, Chaucer, and most important medieval writers used – i.e., *superbia, ira, invidia, avaritia, acedia, gula, luxuria.*) St Thomas Aquinas called these sins *cardinal*, meaning chief or capital, but not *deadly* or mortal. They were final causes which gave rise to other sins, but these seven were not the only sins in his ethic, nor, as Bloomfield points out, "did their commission, if unconfessed, inevitably lead to damnation." However, by the fifteenth and sixteenth centuries, the concepts of capital and deadly sins had merged. See Morton W. Bloomfield, *The Seven Deadly Sins* (East Lansing: Michigan State College 1952). For an account of the concept of accidia up to 1500, see Siegfried Wenzel, *The Sin of Sloth* (Chapel Hill: University of North Carolina Press 1967).

3 Geoffrey Keynes, *Drawings of William Blake* (New York: Dover 1970), plate 55.

4 S. Foster Damon has written, "The Spectre is ruthless in getting its way, and cares nothing for the Individual it obsesses: it will drive him into unhappiness, disaster, and even suicide" (*A Blake Dictionary* [New York: Dutton 1971], 381).

5 F.I. Carpenter, "Spenser's Cave of Despair," *MLN* XII (1897): 129–37.

6 Ibid.

7 This background is documented in detail in Bloomfield, *Seven Deadly Sins*.

8 R. Klibansky, F. Saxl, and E. Panofsky, *Saturn and Melancholy* (New York: Basic Books 1964), 236.
9 Cf. C. Ripa's "Malinconia," in ibid., 405.
10 For Blake's familiarity with these artists, see Jean H. Hagstrum, *William Blake, Poet and Painter* (Chicago: University of Chicago Press 1964). Blake's hunched despair figures are frontal, like the Ripa reproduced in Klibansky or the figure of Jesse on the Sistine ceiling, as distinguished from the semi-profiled figure of Dürer's *Melencholia I*. They differ from the tradition in that they have an exaggerated slump or huddle.
11 See also John E. Grant, "Blake's Designs for *L'Allegro* and *Il Penseroso*," *Blake Newsletter* 16 (Spring 1971): 134.
12 Good examples are evident in the designs to *Night Thoughts*, Nights V & VII.
13 Wenzel, *Sin of Sloth*, 48.
14 In reference to Blake's own personal experience, Morton Paley has explored the connection between the Spectre and a despairing man in "Cowper as Blake's Spectre," *Eighteenth Century Studies* 1 (1968) 236–52.
15 *Milton*, plate 14. Note that Blake uses the same design for Satan in the watercolour *Satan in His Original Glory* and for Milton in plate 13.
16 The figure of Nelson in *The Spiritual Form of Nelson Guiding Leviathan* is demonic, as Morton Paley has discussed in his excellent chap. 7 in *Energy and the Imagination* (Oxford: Clarendon 1970), and despair forms are found surrounding Nelson in this picture. See Paley, plate 3.
17 Bloomfield, *Seven Deadly Sins*, appendix I.
18 "Moreover, Acedia is one of the capital sins ... producing other, even quite distinct, sins" (*New Catholic Encyclopedia* vol. I, 83–4).
19 Damon, *Dictionary*, 104.
20 Frye, *Fearful Symmetry*, 281.
21 This brief catalogue indicates that Blake was adapting into his own myth a tradition whose psychological validity had been thoroughly explored during the Middle Ages and the Renaissance.
22 See also R.E. Simmons, "Urizen: The Symmetry of Fear," in *Blake's Visionary Forms Dramatic*, ed. David V. Erdman and John E. Grant (Princeton: Princeton University Press 1970), 152.
23 "... this Spectre of Tharmas / Is Eternal Death" (FZ I: 5; E 303), and so is Orc (*America* 2: 17; E 52).
24 S. Foster Damon, *Blake's Job* (Providence, RI: Brown University Press 1966), 3.
25 The source for these figures is likely Michelangelo's *Last Judgment*; see Hagstrum, *Blake, Poet and Painter*, 40.
26 Damon, *Dictionary*, 105.

FIVE: THE LEAP

1 Morton D. Paley, *Energy and Imagination: A Study of the Development of Blake's Thought* (Oxford: Clarendon 1970).
2 See NT 1, 2, 97, 114, 217, 268, 291, in *William Blake's Designs for Edward*

Young's Night Thoughts, ed. David V. Erdman, John E. Grant, Edward J. Rose, and Michael J. Tolley, 2 vols. (Oxford: Clarendon 1980).

3 *J* 43.

4 Eudo C. Mason, *The Mind of Henry Fuseli* (London: Routledge & Kegan Paul 1951), 51. A more recent interpretation of Fuseli's design is found in Gert Schiff, *Johann Heinrich Füssli* (Zurich 1973).

5 For an exhaustive account of these influences, see Kathleen Raine, *Blake and Tradition* (Princeton: Princeton University Press 1963). My quotations from Jacob Boehme are from *The Works of Jacob Behmen* (London 1764–81).

6 Donald Ault, *Visionary Physics: Blake's Response to Newton* (Chicago: University of Chicago Press 1974), 13.

7 Ibid., xii.

8 John Grant, "Visions in Vala," in *Blake's Sublime Allegory*, ed. Stuart Curran and Joseph Anthony Wittreich, Jr (Madison: University of Wisconsin Press 1973), 200–2. See also G.E. Bentley, Jr, *Vala or the Four Zoas* (Oxford: Clarendon 1963), 183. Grant's discussion of this particular design is marred by an unusually (for him) confusing mode of observation. He tends to call "prototypical" any figure which even vaguely resembles the one in question. For example, he calls *NT* 139 prototypical of *Vala*, p. 139. He also compares (in n. 61 on p. 200) *Night Thoughts* designs of figures which leap and reach out *in any mode at all*.

9 There has been some controversy about whether this male figure is reclining or rising. See Grant, "Visions in Vala," 146. Grant effectively settles the argument, concluding, "What one *sees* is that the man is rising ..."

10 Ibid., 147.

11 Morton D. Paley, *William Blake* (Oxford: Phaidon 1978), 69; David V. Erdman, *Illuminated Blake* (Garden City: Doubleday 1974), 379; S. Foster Damon, *Blake's Philosophy and Symbols* (Gloucester, Mass.: Peter Smith 1958).

12 Henry Fuseli, *Lectures on Painting* (London: J. Johnson 1801), 5.

13 John Grant, in *Blake's Designs*, ed. Erdman et al., vol. 1, 90, n. 54.

14 Blake's large tempera painting of *The Last Judgment* disappeared shortly after his death. The most convenient place to see reproductions of the surviving designs are in a pamphlet, "Blake's Visions of the Last Judgment," published by *Blake Quarterly* to advertise the MLA Blake Seminar, 28 December 1975. It includes all versions of Blake's pictures of the subject accessible in public collections, including the pen and watercolour versions at Pollock House, Glasgow; Petworth House, Sussex; and Rosenwald Collection, National Gallery, Washington. Also illustrated is the Schiavonetti engraving after Blake of *The Day of Judgment* from Blair's *Grave*, and two drawings of the subject. The booklet also includes a useful discussion by W.J.T. Mitchell, "Blake's Visions of the Last Judgment: Some Problems of Interpretation."

15 For a good discussion of this plate, see W.J.T. Mitchell, *Blake's Composite Art* (Princeton: Princeton University Press 1978), 10–11. It is common to

assume that the title-page depicts an angel and a devil embracing, but I think that the figures are simply male and female and that it is the *marriage* of the title that is emphasized, with its suggested release of desire and energy.

16 Joseph Wicksteed, *Blake's River of Life: Its Poetic Undertones* (Bournemouth, n.d. [1949]).

17 Leopold Damrosch, Jr, is surely correct to see her as a Fate, though he does not think she is cutting anything with her shears. He also thinks that the scene depicts Beulah and that the swimmers will pass through towards the "prophet" (his term for the sun figure). However, Damrosch ignores the scale of the figure: the "prophet" is not in the far distance but quite close, and he is *approaching* the swimmers. Damrosch discusses this picture in *Symbol and Truth in Blake's Myth* (Princeton: Princeton University Press 1980), 231–3.

SIX: THE DANCE

1 Exceptions are some of Blake's fairy-ring dancers.

2 E 544.

3 Cecil Sharp and A.P. Oppe, *The Dance: An Historical Survey of Dance in Europe* (London: Halton and Truscott Smith 1924), 19.

4 Ibid., 28.

5 Frances Rust, *Dance in Society* (London: Routledge & Kegan Paul 1969), 63.

6 Thomas Gray, "A Long Story," in Irene Tayler, *Blake's Illustrations to the Poems of Gray* (Princeton: Princeton University Press 1971), plate 4.

7 Lincoln Kirstein, *Dance: A Short History of Classical Dancing* (New York: T.P. Putnam Sons 1935), 215.

8 Cyril W. Beaumont, trans., in intro. to J.G. Noverre, *Letters on Dancing and Ballet* (London: Beaumont 1930).

9 "I love the jocund dance" of *Poetical Sketches* stands alone as an early expression of pastoral innocence untouched by ambivalence.

10 For example: "Such are the Feminine & Masculine when separated from Man. They call the Rocks Parents of Men, & adore the frowning Chaos Dancing around in howling pain clothed in the bloody veil" (*J* 67: 16–18; E 220).

11 John E. Grant, "The Meaning of Mirth and Her Companions in Blake's Designs for *L'Allegro* and *Il Penseroso*,' *Blake Newsletter* 16 (Winter 1971–72): 190–202. (This is the second of two related articles; the first appeared in Spring 1971: see n. 13.

12 See Marcia R. Pointon, *Milton and English Art* (Toronto: University of Toronto Press 1970), "William Blake and Milton," 135ff.

13 See E.J. Rose, "Blake's Illustrations for *Paradise Lost*, *L'Allegro* and *Il Penseroso:* A Thematic Reading," *Hartford Studies in Literature* 11, no. 1 (1970): 40–67; and John Grant, "Blake's Designs for *L'Allegro* and *Il Penseroso* ...," *Blake Newsletter* 16 (Spring 1971): 117–34. The most useful discussion is

found in Stephen C. Behrendt, "Bright Pilgrimage: William Blake's Designs for *L'Allegro* and *Il Penseroso*," *Milton Studies* 8 (1975): 123–47. Anne Mellor's study, *Blake's Human Form Divine* (Berkeley: University of California Press 1974), also discusses these designs, 270–85.

14 Martin Butlin, *William Blake* (London: Tate Gallery 1978), 120.

15 Behrendt, "Bright Pilgrimage," 136.

16 Pointon, *Milton and English Art*, 47 and xxxvi.

17 For a list of these, which include designs by Fuseli, Westall, Hayman, Smirke, Martin, etc., see Stephen C. Behrendt, "The Mental Contest: Blake's *Comus* Designs," *Blake Studies* 8, no. 1 (1978): 67.

18 Angus Fletcher, *The Transcendental Masque* (Ithaca: Cornell University Press 1971), "A Note on Blake's Illustrations for Comus," 253–6.

19 Behrendt, "Bright Pilgrimage," 65.

20 Ibid., 74.

21 Fletcher, *Transcendental Masque*, 255. My argument here will add further "minute particulars" to some suggestive statements of Fletcher, whose brief (three-page) comparison of Blake's two sets of designs grasps the essential meaning of the illustrations.

22 Ibid., 254.

23 Irene Tayler, "Say First! What Mov'd Blake?: Blake's *Comus* Designs and *Milton*," in *Blake's Sublime Allegory*, ed. Stuart Curran and Joseph A. Wittreich, Jr (Madison: University of Wisconsin Press 1973), 233–58.

24 Fletcher, *Transcendental Masque*, 212–13.

25 Ibid., 255.

26 Ibid., 116–17.

27 See Robert Essick, *William Blake Printmaker* (Princeton: Princeton University Press 1980), 70–8, for the definitive account of the development of this design.

28 Ibid., 72.

29 See also Joseph Anthony Wittreich, Jr, *Angel of Apocalypse: Blake's Idea of Milton* (Madison: University of Wisconsin Press 1975).

COMMENTARY: *THE FALL OF MAN*

1 See David Bindman, *Blake as an Artist* (Oxford: Phaidon 1977), 165–9, for a useful account of the versions of the *Last Judgment*. See also chap. 5 above, no. 14.

2 See Butlin, *Paintings and Drawings: Plates*, 467. The painting measures 19 × 15-1/2 in. (48.3 × 38.7).

3 Bindman, *Blake as an Artist*, 165–6.

4 See other examples in figures 1–5.

5 S. Foster Damon, *A Blake Dictionary* (New York: E.P. Dutton 1971).

6 J.B. Trapp, "The Iconography of the Fall of Man," in *Approaches to Paradise Lost: The York Tercentenary Lectures* (London: Edward Arnold 1968).

7 For this insight (which I have applied to this picture) I am indebted to James Boyd Brown's PHD dissertation, "The History of an Illusion: The

Meaning of the Zoas in Blake's *The Four Zoas*" (York University, Toronto 1983).

8 See *Job* 1, *Thus did Job continually*. The words "the Letter Killeth the Spirit giveth Life" are part of the design. See S. Foster Damon, *Blake's Job* (Providence: RI: Brown University Press 1966), 12.

CONCLUSION

1 Norman Bryson, *Word and Image* (Cambridge: Cambridge University Press 1981), 5.

2 See David Bindman's article in *Blake in His Time*, ed. Robert N. Essick and Donald Pearce (Bloomington: Indiana University Press 1978), 92.

3 Ibid., 98.

4 George Cumberland, *An Essay on the Utility of Collecting the Best Works of the Ancient Engravers of the Italian School ...* (London 1827), 15.

Index

Index

Index

This book was designed by William Rueter RCA, who also created the display letterform, based on Blake's early engraved lettering, especially for this volume. The book was printed by University of Toronto Press.